AN INTRODUCTION TO

CACTI

by Danny Schuster

AN INTRODUCTION TO

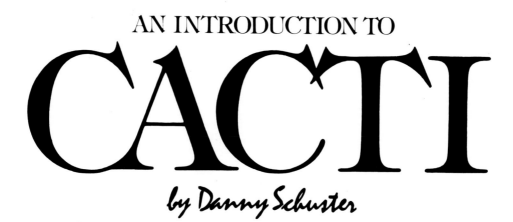

CACTI

by Danny Schuster

BLANDFORD PRESS
POOLE • DORSET

First published in the U.K. 1984 by Blandford Press,
Link House, Poole, Dorset BH15 ILL

Distributed in the United States by
Sterling Publishing Co., Inc.,
2 Park Avenue, New York, N.Y. 10016

British Library Cataloguing in Publication Data
Schuster, Danny
An introduction to cacti.
1. Cactus—New Zealand
I. Title
583'.47'09931   QK495.C11

ISBN 0 7137 1499 9

First Published 1983 by Bascands Limited
145–153 Kilmore Street
Christchurch
New Zealand

Designed by Jaap Koster
Colour separations and filmwork by Bascands,
Christchurch
Typeset by Quickset Platemakers,
Christchurch
Printed in Singapore by Kyodo-Shing Loong

Foreword

An Introduction to Cacti is a practical book which should be in every cactophile's library. It will prove most useful both to beginners and to advanced collectors. There is an abundance of literature about growing cacti, but books such as this, both comprehensive and beautifully presented, are 'conspicuous by their rarity'.

It is well illustrated with superb colour reproductions which are very true to colour and are of excellent sharpness, showing all parts of the plants and flowers in great detail. So many books dealing with cacti unfortunately fail to reproduce the true flower colours of the plants named and described.

The chapter dealing with propagation is very important. All hobbyists *should* be able to raise cacti from seed. To be able to say proudly that such and such a plant has been raised from seed gives one an inner glow of having achieved something.

Every cactophile should have the ability to undertake grafting. However, grafting should be undertaken with a great deal of discretion. When one masters the art, there is a great temptation to graft 'everything in sight'. All grafts should be made for a reason. If a plant is very slow-growing, or is difficult to grow on its own roots under our conditions, it may be advisable to graft it; or a plant could be about to die and be difficult to reroot from a cutting or offset and one could, in order to save it, resort to grafting.

While grafting should be performed during spring and summer, plants can, in fact, be grafted at any time of the year. I have seen cacti, which were on the point of dying, grafted in the middle of winter, and saved because the collector was bold enough to graft. Cacti which are very sick in mid winter are going to die anyway, so why not endeavour to save them by grafting?

Virtually all of the plants described here can be purchased as seedlings, or can be grown from seed obtainable from the specialist suppliers.

N.M. STOW

New Zealand Cactus and Succulent Society

Contents

Introduction

Why grow cacti? A question which is often asked by anyone seeing for the first time collections of plants resembling balls of spines displayed on a windowsill, in a garden or in a glasshouse. The answer is often a matter of simple impulse although, to a cacti collector, no other species of flowering plant is more fascinating.

Most 'cactophiles' or cacti lovers are introduced to their hobby early in life. Usually a friend gives them an offset of an unusually fierce looking plant with sharp spines and an exotic name like *Opuntia* or *Echinopsis*. The young recipient is unaware, at the time, that a single plant will probably lead him to develop a keen interest in an ever-growing collection of different cacti. Their great adaptibility to adverse conditions, their seemingly unending variation in shape and colour and, not least, the exotic beauty of their flowers, will capture him for life.

During the first year or so, the plant's proud owners will discover that many of the myths about cacti are no more than that, myths. That, despite popular belief, their spines are not poisonous and that flowering occurs with great regularity — not just once every seven years. That, in fact, cacti are hardy and can occupy a minimum of space and that, as a result of their resilient nature, these remarkable plants need little attention or specialised care. A profusion of flowers and colourful spines have more than once converted a sceptic into a dedicated collector.

With the space limitations of an average contemporary home or flat — with or without a garden — the area available for plants is rapidly decreasing. Many of the larger old-fashioned house-plants require a great deal of attention and demand conditions that are lacking in modern houses. Cacti, on the other hand, seem to thrive in adverse conditions and do not suffer from lack of space and limited attention. Few, if any, plant types can match cacti in their ability to convert a small window-sill into an exotic garden of shapes, rich in colour and with a profusion of flowers from mid winter through to the heat of summer.

Possibly the most convenient aspect of growing cacti as a house-plant is that they are hardy and will survive for great lengths of time without watering. Many a grower can return home from a holiday of three or more weeks to find his cacti plants in a better condition than when he left! In fact, most cacti that suffer at the hand of their owners are killed by kindness — for example excessive repotting or watering.

As will be seen in the introductory chapters, the conditions and care under which most cacti will thrive are simple. Once established on a sunny window, porch or sheltered garden corner, cacti will continue to grow and flower with the minimum of attention.

For the professional grower and nurseryman, cacti provide an ideal plant. Their ease of propagation, combined with a minimum space requirement and rapid growth to saleable, mature plants, are all great advantages.

The hybridisation of older types and 'new finds' of cacti in the Americas provide established collectors with the continuing interest of adding to their chosen selections. A steadily growing and now widespread interest in cacti is best shown by the rapidly increasing number of societies and clubs in all countries. The number of specialised cacti-growing nurseries in the UK, the USA, Europe, Australasia and Japan is also increasing.

Membership of a society provides the newcomer to the world of cacti with an opportunity to learn about these fascinating plants — in an informal atmosphere of friendship with more experienced growers — and also the opportunity to visit private collections. The generosity of cacti collectors is legendary and, as many before me, I owe a great debt of gratitude to many such hobbyists in Europe and Australasia. Without their advice, guidance and assistance, and without their generosity with plants over the past two decades, my own little collection, or this book, would not have been possible.

A debt of gratitude, as well, to G. Barker, Jaap Koster and Graham Steans, all skilful photographers of plants who have applied their craft with dedication to record the fascinating beauty of cacti plants in flower. Some of the plants shown are from my own collection, others are from collections of vastly more experienced growers, such as Mr N. Stow and Mr G. Barker of Christchurch.

Finally, I owe a debt of gratitude to my editor, Michael ffolliott-Foster, for his help and advice.

Christchurch, June 1983

Natural Distribution

From the morphology of cacti, with their simply structured flowers, and from the unique distribution of their genera in parts of the North and South American continent, there is an indication that members of the cacti family (*Cactaceae*) are related to some of the oldest plants in that continent. Cacti plants are '*dicotyledonous*' — the seedlings have two leaves, and the seed pod, 'fruit', is a one-celled berry. All cacti flowers have petals above the seed-bearing pod, and their stigma is divided into a number of lobes. All plants have areolae from which spines, wool and sometimes flowers originate.

The plants are perennial, that is to say they live for a number of years and do not die after flowering and the seasonal production of seeds. More recent studies of climatic changes, and their effect on flora in South America (Backeberg 1976), explain in greater detail the pattern of separate distribution and development of many cacti genera. It seems reasonable to assume that in the past, during a period with more favourable climatic conditions, the natural spread of distribution was much greater than in recent times. The hitherto widespread and uninterrupted distribution of related genera has gradually changed to the more isolated patterns of today. A cooler and less humid climate has, in many areas, forced cacti types to retreat in a general direction from south to north. In regions where the climatic changes occurred over a long period, sometimes involving thousands of years, many genera of cacti adapted well to the changes.

The morphological reduction of leaves to spines and glochids, as seen clearly with *Opuntias* and *Peireskiopsis*, are examples of such adaptations. The reduction of plant stems to a thickened body of 'cereoid' or 'globular' shape ensures that moisture loss is kept to a minimum. This decline in water loss because of reduced transpiration, combined with the reservoir of water stored in the tissues of the thickened body and roots, allow cacti to survive in the arid conditions found in many parts of the Americas .

Further marked differences in cacti genera occurred as a result of dramatic changes in the landscape, such as the volcanic rise of the Andes which effectively separated the ancestral cacti types of Chile.

Natural hybridisation, resulting from the cross-pollination of related genera, is a continuing process even today, and no doubt will continue in the future to complicate all attempts to provide a definitive classification of cacti.

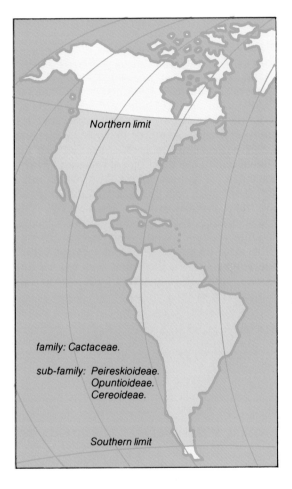

Fig. 1. The Distribution of Cacti in their Natural Habitat. (after Backeberg 1976).

Countries in which the majority of cacti are found: the USA, Mexico, Cuba, the West Indies, Honduras, Chile, Bolivia, Uruguay, Paraguay, Peru, Guatemala, Ecuador, Brazil and Argentina.

The natural distribution of cacti extends from the northern limits of the USA / Canada border,

9

through Central America and the West Indies into the South American sub-continent, reaching its southern limit in Brazil and Argentina. Fig. 1 shows the widespread distribution of cacti in the Americas.**

Natural Environment

The wide-ranging variations of soil types and climates which form the natural habitat of cacti demonstrate the adaptibility of these remarkable plants. The 'cereoid' (columnar), 'globular' (rounded) and 'epiphytic' (segmented) cacti are found in the arid deserts of the USA, Mexico and Chile; on the inhospitable mountain slopes of the Andes and in the sub-tropical forests of Brazil. As these are the environments in which cacti thrive, the most successful conditions for growing them, indoors or in the garden, will in all major aspects duplicate the soil and climatic characteristics of their native habitat. Unless otherwise specified — as in *Zygocactus, Melocactus* etc — the types selected for this book will grow and flower well if given the following basic conditions:

- A coarse soil mix which allows for rapid water drainage and easy root penetration.

- A soil type that has a slightly acid pH reaction, low humus content and an ample supply of potassium and phosphorus.

- A position with plentiful sun and warmth, combined with regular watering during the period of active growth and flowering.

- A cool and dry 'rest' with no watering during the inactive winter months. Lack of moisture during the winter rest periods is tempered by misting the plants with water during the fine days to ensure that they remain healthy.

- A basic protection from damage by sun, excessive heat or frost, and the prevention of insect infestation.

The conditions for more detailed care of individual cacti plants, grown indoors or in the garden, are given in Chapter 2. However, the requirements already referred to should be used as a general guideline.

** *More recent studies of the divergent characteristics of species within the* **Rhipsalis** *genus of tropical, epiphytic cacti, suggest that samples found in the southern parts of Africa, Madagascar and Ceylon are native populations rather than modern introductions as was previously thought. The native habitat of* **Rhipsalis** *(Gartn), i.e.* **R.cassutha, R.corraloides, R.fasciculata, R.horrida, R.lindbergiana, R.madagascarensis, R.pilosa, R.prismatica, R.saxicola** *species therefore remains a matter to be resolved.*

Light

Under outdoor conditions, most cacti are best suited to full light and a sunny position. Many genera are well adapted to thrive in conditions of great light intensity and summer heat. Fine wool, dense spines and deeply carved ribs act as a protection against sun rays and excessive light. A sheltered verandah, or the sun-exposed corner of a garden are well suited to duplicating natural conditions.

Covering garden soil around the base of plants with a coarse gravel of light colour will reflect much of the light received and will also ensure that the soil near the plants is kept dry. It should be noted that cacti will thrive better under the harsher summer conditions of an outdoor garden. Their growth will be slower but more sturdy, plants will flower more freely and will withstand greater amounts of direct sun without damage from sunburn.

Plants raised and grown indoors, or in glasshouses, will grow faster and have a better appearance but will also be more sensitive to sunburn during the hot periods of midsummer.

An excessive build-up of heat in glass covered areas can be avoided by shading and regular ventilation. The brown scarring of the surface tissues of cacti is caused by excessive sunlight and heat and, although this rarely damages older plants, it can make them less visually attractive.

Alternatively, insufficient light will cause cacti to display pale colouration and result in an elongation of the growing tip and poor flowering. Enforced winter growth — caused by excessive warmth and winter watering — should be avoided, except for the young seedlings which are best raised in a glasshouse under improved or supplemented light.

The subtropical, epiphytic cacti (*Schlumbergera, Zygocactus* and others), favour semi-shade during the period of summer growth. The required dispersed light and less intense heat, combined with greater humidity, can be found under the branches of larger trees, partly covered verandahs or similar locations. The large and colourful flowers of these tropical cacti will develop best on the hardened, well-coloured segments which have, under open-air conditions, had a chance to mature in the semi-shade.

Conditions of more or less constant heat and good light intensity will support flowering in the cooler months of the year. Sudden changes of temperature, moisture and light, will often result in flower-bud drop or poor coloration of flowers.

All cacti seedlings should be shielded from full sun until they have developed spines to provide protection. Some genera will benefit from slightly shaded positions, for example *Gymnocalycium*, *Parodia* and others. The flowering of such cacti when grown in a glasshouse will be improved by placing them in a cool position away from direct sunlight. In the generally cooler conditions of a garden, shade will be less critical.

Temperature

In their natural environment of America (North and South) cacti experience a temperature range which is typified by cool, dry winters and warm springs. Spring rains are followed by dry, hot summers and the growing cycle for most varieties reflect these conditions. Cacti are well adapted to gain the maximum advantage from any water which is available during the spring, and this results in a rapid swelling of the body and the appearance of flowers. During the hot part of the summer, cacti retain moisture in their tissues for long periods. Shrivelling and reduced tension in body-surface tissue limits the moisture loss to a minimum and the combination of spines and hair/wool provides the required shade from direct sunlight.

Winters are usually cold and dry. Some genera of cacti (*Cereus*, *Espostoa* etc) are found in areas with winter frost although, with decreasing temperature, their resistance to excess moisture in the soil and atmosphere is decreased. Also, under natural conditions, cacti plants undergo a period of hardening in late summer and autumn. Under the artificial conditions of cultivation, the growing season is extended well into the autumn and it is important to assist the hardening of plants by reducing the frequency of watering, and by ventilation at night.

Hardened plants will be better able to withstand the colder winter months. In districts with severe winter frosts ($-3°C$ or greater), further protection from frost may be required. Glasshouse plants can benefit from improved insulation and limited heating, outdoor plants from being covered or brought indoors. In countries with severe winters (Northern Europe, Canada), plants are often taken out of the soil and stored, carefully wrapped in paper for protection, and placed inside boxes. Cacti in these conditions can be kept in the cool, dry environment of a cellar until the warmer months of spring when they are repotted and placed in their summer position, see Fig. 2.

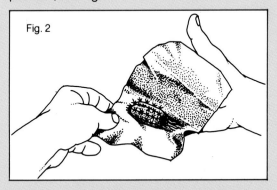

Fig. 2

Some larger specimens of columnar cacti grown in gardens (*Trichocereus*, *Oreocereus* etc), can withstand mild frosts without damage, providing the roots and the base of each plant are dry. Covering the soil and the base of the plant with mulched straw provides a suitable frost protection. Outdoor cacti, planted in positions exposed to winter rain, have a low tolerance to winter frosts.

As stated earlier, the over-heating of poorly ventilated glasshouses can cause brown scarring in cacti and, except on wet or cold days, ventilators should be kept open during the summer and autumn periods. The frequent ventilation of glasshouses during fine, sunny days in winter is also recommended so as to avoid a build-up of stale air which could favour the spread of insect infestations and mould. Excessive heat and moisture build-up in glasshouses during winter could also lead to premature winter growth, and to cacti having distorted shapes.

Moisture and Watering
Regular watering should be restricted to the months when there is visible, active growth of plants. In principle, watering to 'run-off point' once or twice a week is better than watering daily. Soils, rather than being kept wet, should be given time to dry out between watering. Water should be applied carefully to the soil surface, keeping the body of the cactus dry. Morning

watering is preferable, though late afternoon is also suitable, providing that the soil surface has time to dry out before the cool part of the evening. Watering during the greatest heat of the day should be avoided. If it becomes necessary, humidity can safely be increased by plant misting or spraying water over the glasshouse floor.

Problems associated with excessive heat and humidity rarely arise with plants grown in a suitable part of a garden, a window-sill or porch. The watering patterns in such positions should resemble those outlined for glasshouses — the soil again being allowed to dry out between waterings. It should be remembered that potted cacti will require more regular watering than plants grown in larger volumes of soil in gardens or soil-filled benches.

In the early spring it is safer not to water cacti until there is some visible growth of shiny tips, new spines or flower buds.

Freshly potted plants should not be watered until the roots have had time to grow, usually a week or two after planting. Obvious growth is again a safe indicator of the need to water.

Towards the end of the growing season, watering should be gradually decreased until the plants are hardened sufficiently for their dry, winter rest. Watering can be stopped altogether during the winter and the occasional misting of plants will prove sufficient to avoid shrivelling. Shrivelling, it is of interest to note, has no detrimental or lasting effect on cacti. It is caused by gradual moisture loss and can be rapidly reversed in the spring. Plants that have not been allowed to shrivel excessively during the winter appear more attractive and begin their active growth and flowering earlier in the spring.

Water used for cacti should, ideally, have a slightly acid pH reaction, be close to air temperature and have an abundance of dissolved oxygen. These conditions can be achieved by storing rain water. When this is not convenient, tap water, with its usually high pH value (alkaline), can be suitably adjusted by adding a few drops of sulphuric acid, using litmus paper as an indicator — acid and litmus paper kits can be obtained from a chemist's shop. The litmus paper shows, by simple changes in colour, the pH value of the water which is being tested and the acid is then added, drop by drop, until the required neutral range is attained.

Soil Mix and Fertilisers

Many growers prepare their own 'special' soil mix and opinions vary as to which is ideal for this or that type of cacti. Despite differing opinions, the more successful growers use a soil which is well drained, thus coarse; warms up readily in the sun; allows for easy root penetration and repotting; contains low levels of nitrogen and has balanced levels of other nutrients. In texture, suitable soil mixes range from coarse, medium coarse, medium coarse enriched with humus to fine; the last being best suited to seedlings. A humus-enriched, medium coarse mix is often used for the tropical, epiphytic types sometimes called 'orchid cacti' (*Zygocactus* and others). Moss can be added to this mix to improve its moisture-holding capability, thus making it suitable for use in hanging baskets.

Fine Soil Mix

A propagating mixture which usually consists of one part sharp sand to two parts well-matured, sieved compost from peat or leaf mulch. When steamed or chemically sterilised, this fine textured soil is best suited to raising young cacti seedlings or growing small plants. Usually no fertiliser is required as sufficient nutrients for early growth are already present. Some commerical growers use nitrogen-rich fertilisers during watering, or in the form of a spray to speed-up the growth of young seedlings. Caution, however, is advised as, without experience, this procedure can lead to distortions of plant shape, insufficient hardening of tissues and plant loss (see Chapter 3).

Medium Coarse Soil Mix
with or without, Humus Enrichment

A good composition suitable for most of the taller, vigorously growing cacti (*Cereoid*, *Lobivoid*, *Opuntia* etc). It is also used for plants with a stout tap root (*Copiapoa*, some *Mammillaria* and similar genera). A medium coarse soil mix, without humus enrichment, may be made from peat (30%), roughly sieved garden soil, or mature leaf mulch (30%) and coarse gravel or crushed brick (40%). A handful of inorganic fertiliser (granulated, slow-release types are preferable), rich in potassium and phosphorus, may be added to each 10kg bag of mix. Small amounts of Paradichlor-benzene crystals, as a protection against root mealy bug, can also be added (see Chapter 3).

As the trade names and composition of fertilisers vary from place to place, consult a local supplier or nursery for details of the most suitable types that are available.

To increase the humus and moisture retention of this soil — for growing epiphytic cacti — halve the quantity of coarse gravel or crushed brick and substitute an equal amount (20%) of sphagnum moss or well-composed peat moss.

Coarse Soil Mix

A suitable blend for all Mexican or American desert cacti of spherical shape, or for the small, slow-growing genera from Chile, Argentina and Bolivia. The coarse soil texture will allow for a rapid drainage of water and, depending on the container used, the frequency of summer watering will be increased. A coarse soil mix may be made up from coarse gravel or crushed brick (50%), peat (25%) and roughly sieved, mature compost (leaf mulch 25%). A handful (250-300g) of inorganic fertiliser, as described for medium coarse soils, should be added for each 10kg of soil mix. Mealy bug protection crystals, as before, are also used.

Hydroponic* Culture and Soils

The raising of young plants — and the maintaining of larger collections — under conditions of hydroponic culture have advantages when compared to more traditional methods. Hydroponic culture is best suited to larger, commercial nurseries or to cacti collectors — to conditions where detailed and continuous attention can be given to plant health and nutrition.

Hydroponic culture basically consists of a large raised bed which has been filled with inert soil, sharp sand, crushed brick (gravel) etc, and through which a solution of nutrients is circulated at regular intervals. Young seedlings may be

---

* Although the term hydroponic is used throughout, it should be realised that all references are to a semi-hydroponic condition, consisting of growing media — for example gravel — and a hydroponic, nutrient solution.

placed in such raised beds at an early stage and can be removed, potted and sold, when they reach a mature size.

A combination of ideal nutrients and disease control results in a more rapid development of young plants and an excellent success rate with seedlings. The expense of setting up a hydroponic bench deters many small growers and private collectors, despite the fact that hydroponic culture saves considerable amounts of time and money which can otherwise be spent on repotting and on new soil mixes.

Hydroponic benches also create considerably safer conditions for raising seedlings and for maintaining mature plants.

When large collections of cacti are grown on a hydroponic bench it is advisable to group together plants with similar moisture / nutrient requirements or, at least, to separate plants with differing growing cycles onto separate parts of the bench. The placement of cacti with regard to their future growth is also important, as this will avoid the necessity of re-establishing grown plants at a later stage.

A typical, hydroponic bench (see Fig. 3) could consist of a raised bed — with sides of sufficient depth to accommodate seedlings (20-25cm), or mature plants (40-50cm) — constructed from permanent, non-corrosive materials. Drainage outlets from the bottom of the bench may be connected by plastic piping to a container of nutrient solution below the bench.

The raised bed is filled with fine gravel or a similar inert medium — as previously indicated — and nutrient solution is supplied to the mix by a small pump which pipes the liquid from a reservoir. The reservoir — with a predetermined capacity sufficient for its purpose — is kept below the bench. The nutrients are supplied to each plant, or section of the bench, by a network of small plastic tubes which provide 'drip feed' delivery.

Surplus nutrient solution is drained back into the reservoir and recycled for further use. It is important that the nutrient solution is checked periodically and adjusted, if necessary, to the correct strength.

Various hydroponic solutions — with a balanced nutrient content of low pH value — are suitable. In some countries already prepared solutions are available.

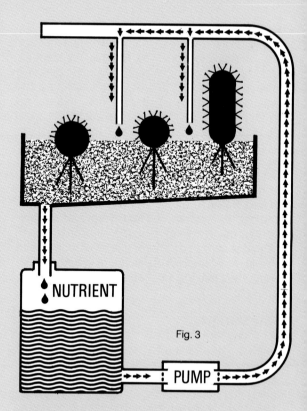

Fig. 3

Generally, cacti will grow well in solutions containing equal amounts of nitrogen, potassium and phosphorus, to which amounts of minor nutrients have been added. For the best results, discuss your likely requirements with a local nursery or fertiliser supplier and obtain detailed advice on the solutions and inorganic fertilisers that are available in your area.

Containers for Growing Cacti

For many years clay pots have traditionally been used for cacti. More recently, lighter and cheaper plastic pots have come to be used for solitary plants or for mini-gardens. The advantages of non-porous, plastic pots or painted metal tins include a reduction in moisture loss and a more even distribution of root systems throughout the available soil.

It should be remembered that containers used for cacti plants should never be excessively large and that yearly repotting of the rapidly growing plants is preferable to the use of outsized pots. Frequent repotting of young plants will speed up their development, and pots of two-to-three times the diameter of the young plant are sufficient to maintain healthy growth. Mature, full-sized plants should be repotted less frequently, and usually only into pots of the same or a slightly larger size. When metal tins are used, these should be painted with a non-toxic paint to prevent rust.

Larger containers and trays can be used with success to create mini-gardens. Some four to six different cacti are usually planted together in such gardens. The contrast between the shapes and colours of plants can be complemented by the use of drift-wood or other natural objects (stones, gravel etc) to isolate individual plants and generally enhance visual appeal. The positioning of taller cacti at the back and smaller, globular plants at the front, allows for future plant growth and for a greater visual impact. If plants have been correctly spaced, the need for frequent repotting may be avoided and mini-gardens can be grown for a number of years in the same container.

Planting and Re-planting of Cacti in Small Containers

When placing a plant in a pot or a tray, the base of the container should be filled with coarse gravel to cover the drainage hole so that excess water can escape with relative freedom (see Fig. 4). Sufficient soil is then placed in the container to cover the roots of the plant to the point where they join the body (to protect the spines, and the grower's hands, rolled paper or a piece of cloth may be used to hold the plant in position, see Fig. 5).

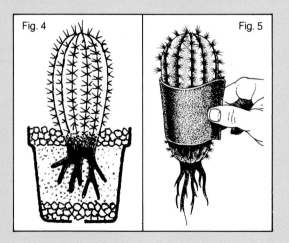

Fig. 4   Fig. 5

After gently firming the soil near the plant and at the edge of the container, coarse gravel is added to cover the soil and the base of the plant. When removing a plant from an old container, during repotting or for any other reason, care must be taken not to disturb the ball of roots to any great degree. However, dead or diseased roots should be cut off with a sharp knife.

Growing Cacti in Large Trays and Benches

Grouping a collection of plants in large trays or on raised benches can have advantages over the more conventional growing of cacti in pots or other small containers. In addition to the increased visual appeal of grouped plants, with differing colours and shapes growing naturally rather than in solitary isolation, repotting, maintenance and the need for frequent watering is greatly reduced.

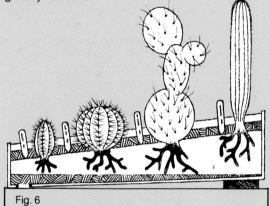

Fig. 6

With selective arrangement, the taller columnar types towards the back and the smaller, globular varieties to the front, the plants should have enough space to reach three or four times their original planting size. The spaces between the plants can be filled with stones, drift-wood, or similar decorative objects which blend with their surroundings. Under these conditions it is only necessary to repot plants every 7-10 years (see Fig. 6).

Some important points to remember when planting and maintaining a large cacti garden include:

- Ensuring that the bench supports are strong enough to carry the full weight of soil, plants and stones.

- Making sure that the planting depth of the tray or bench allows for the development of a strong root system. A minimum of 30-50cm depth will probably be required.

- Ensuring that all trays and benches are constructed from permanent, non-corrosive materials such as wood, plastic, painted metal etc.

- Providing for adequate water by ensuring that the drainage holes are sited in the lowest parts of the bench or tray — slightly elevating (3-5°) the rear support section will assist rapid drainage.

- Remembering that when filling a bench with soil mix a layer of gravel 5cm deep at the base will assist drainage. A further layer of gravel may then be placed on top of the soil after planting to keep the plants dry and free from soil splashing during watering. The mix customarily used is a medium coarse type which suits most cacti. A dressing of inorganic fertiliser can be added each year at the time of spring watering.

- Delaying any watering of the planted bench until the plants show visible signs of growth. Watering is then maintained during the spring/summer months at weekly to ten-day intervals — depending on plant growth and variations in temperature. Allow the soil to dry out between watering and avoid splashing the plants. Water should be applied gently to the gravel covering of the soil until run-off is observed from the drainage holes. During the winter, on sunny days, use a fine misting of water to avoid excessive shrivelling of mature plants.

- Pre-determining which types of cacti go best together to give the greatest possible contrast in shape and colour of the body, spines and flowers.

- Placing small plastic or metal labels near each plant to assist with easy identification.

Growing Cacti on Window-sills and Plant Stands
A hardy nature and small size makes many cacti plants very suitable for cultivation in the restricted space of a window-sill or on a small plant stand. Their distinctive apearance contrasts well with other house-plants.

Ideal indoor positions will provide:

- Plenty of light with direct exposure to the sun for at least a few hours each day.

- Easy access to individual plants for watering during the growth period.

- A cool position with good exposure to light during the winter months.

- Enough space, if required, to accommodate trays or larger pots planted as mini-gardens to produce a greater visual effect with several cacti grouped together.

- Protection from excessive changes in temperature: plants on window-sills should be positioned so that curtains, when drawn, can come between them and the glass surface of the window.

Growing Cacti in a Sun-room or Porch
A sun-room, or the sheltered section of a porch or verandah often provide an ideal environment for most cacti. In addition to solitary plants in pots, there is often enough room for trays or small benches in which mini-gardens can be established. Hanging baskets, planted with epiphytic cacti (*Zygocactus*) can, as well, be displayed with great visual impact.

The wintering of cacti in a sun-room or sheltered porch should provide no problems for even the least experienced grower — providing the plants have had a chance, with increased ventilation and reduced watering, to harden off in autumn.

In regions with severe winter frosts some additional protection — covering the plants, at night only, with a plastic frame or paper — may be required for outdoor positions. Smaller plants, of course, can simply be brought indoors until the danger of severe frosts is over.

Growing Cacti in Outdoor Gardens
Some of the most prolifically flowering and colourful cacti I have seen were grown in outdoor gardens. The somewhat harsher environment of open-air cultivation is considered, by many growers, to be ideal for the best development of spines, body shape and flowers. This includes the smaller, globular types of *Lobivia*, *Echinopsis*, *Gymnocalycium*, *Acanthocalycium* and *Notocactus*, as well as the columnar cereoid types: *Cleistocactus*, *Cereus*, *Trichocereus*, *Helianthocereus* and *Oreocereus*. The softer bodied, small cacti: *Mammillaria*, *Rebutia*, *Astrophytum*, *Coryphantha*, *Neochilenia* and *Parodia* can also be successfully grown outdoors, providing some form of additional protection from frost and rain is available. Polythene frames or similar semi-permanent structures can provide the required protection.

Good conditions for the establishment and care of outdoor cacti include:

● Providing a well-drained soil profile (a depth of 50 to 75cm), with a suitable base which enables water to drain away from the roots of the plants. Natural drainage, in many gardens, can be improved by raising the soil bed — in which the cacti have been planted — above the surrounding general level of the garden. A supporting wall of bricks or timber can be used for this purpose. Additionally, a layer of coarse gravel placed around the base of the plants could provide a further means of draining surplus water away from the roots.

● The use of average garden soil, providing that it is supplemented by sand, peat and gravel to provide a medium coarse soil mix. Inorganic fertilisers can be added, at a rate of one handful per square metre, to the soil prior to planting.

● Stretching a sheet of polythene over the soil prior to planting to prevent weed growth among the plants during the years to come. Cacti can then be planted through holes in the polythene and the area between plants covered with a layer of coarse gravel.

● Placing tall, cereoid cacti towards the back of the garden — with stakes or similar supports to provide protection from wind damage. Large stones or driftwood can be placed among the plants to give the garden a natural appearance.

● Raising separate parts of the garden to differing levels — with the aid of bricks or a stone wall — can highlight individual groups of cacti and can add greater visual appeal to the whole area.

● Making provision for some protection from frosts or direct rain in more exposed locations — existing structures, walls or fences can be utilised, as well as the temporary use, in winter, of polythene frames or mulching materials (straw etc).

● Watering, which should be limited to periods of prolonged dry weather during the summer months when cacti benefit from additional moisture during their active growth and flowering period. Care should be taken to avoid splashing the plants with water, as this could lead to rotting and the subsequent loss of plants.

Growing Cacti in Frames or Glasshouses
Many of the larger cacti collections are housed under the permanent protection of polythene or glass frames, or in glasshouses. Although expensive, these structures provide controlled growing conditions in areas where climatic conditions vary considerably between summer and winter. The controlled conditions of a frame or glasshouse also make it possible to raise cacti plants from seed or to grow sensitive types such

as *Melocactus* and others which could not be grown outdoors. Generally, plants are grown in pots which are arranged on shelves or tables. Some growers prefer to raise plants in groups, planting them directly in raised benches or in the soil on the glasshouse floor.

The tall, columnar cacti are usually planted in the centre, or underneath the highest section of a glasshouse or frame, where they can reach their maximum possible size. The smaller, globular cacti are then placed on benches along the structure's sides so as to receive an ample amount of light and direct sun. A small area of the glasshouse or frame is also reserved for storage, for repotting and for young plants which have been raised from seed.

Spare headroom can be utilised by planting cacti in hanging baskets.

Major requirements for the successful culture of cacti in covered frames and glasshouses include:

● An avoidance of overheating and damage from sunburn by the use of ventilation and shading.

   A simple form of shading can be achieved by spraying the outside of the structure with a lime-water solution. This can be renewed each spring, or as required. Shading cloths, attached to the inside of the structure, provide a more permanent protection and these can be removed in winter to increase the amount of light available to the plants. Ventilators can often be left open throughout the summer, except for cold or windy days.

Ventilators should be used during fine days, even in winter, to prevent an accumulation of stale air which would favour the spread of insects and of mould diseases.

● The design of structures — glasshouses, polythene frames etc — should allow for plants to be positioned so that there is easy access for watering and inspection. Poorly watered plants, unsprayed or uncared for — or out of reach — are often lost to pests or disease. The atmosphere around cacti, within a totally covered environment, favours the spread of insects and diseases. Plants should be carefully inspected at regular intervals, and this should be combined with an overall spraying programme if plants are to remain healthy and undamaged (see Chapter 3 for recommended sprays).

● Improved insulation. This or a limited amount of heating may be required in districts with severe winter frosts. Winter heating should be restricted to frost periods and should be regulated so that temperatures do not fall below 5-10°C. Excessive heat in winter could lead to renewed plant growth which, in turn, would result in greater frost susceptibility and the misshaping of cacti forms. It is important to remember that winter heating also results in the air around the plants becoming dried and misting should be used to prevent excessive shrivelling.

Propagation by Offsets and Stem Segments

A small number of new plants can be raised each year by separating the new offsets and stem segments from older plants. Many genera of cacti form such offsets from the base or sides of their body. In others the mature sections of stem can be separated by a sharp knife and planted in a new pot to strike roots (see Fig. 8a).

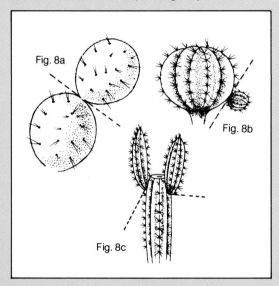

Fig. 8a

Fig. 8b

Fig. 8c

With some, like *Rebutia* or *Echinopsis*, the cushion of individual heads can be separated and replanted to form new colonies (see Fig. 8b).

The taller, cereoid cacti of *Cereus*, *Trichocereus* and similar genera may not readily form new offsets, although they can be forced to do so by the removal of their growing tip or upper section. Offsets will then form rapidly on the remaining 'mother plant' section, and such plants can become a source of new plant material for years to come. Growers, who have a need for a regular supply of rootstock material for grafting with *Peireskiopsis* or *Trichocereus* types, use this 'mother plant' technique with success (see Fig. 8c).

It should be remembered that newly separated sections or offsets should be allowed to heal by drying off in the sun prior to repotting in order to avoid any rotting of the freshly cut surface. Light dusting with sulphur powder or a similar sanitising agent is used to prevent infection by moulds. However, the offsets, or the cut surface on a rootstock plant intended for grafting, should be used fresh and the area of cut must not be allowed to dry out before the union is made.

Propagation of Cacti by Seed

The large-scale propagation of cacti, by commercial nurseries or larger growers, can only be achieved by using seed. Seeds are sold by specialised seed firms (see Appendix 2), or can be gathered from plants in a grower's collection. Although raising plants on a large scale from seed involves time-consuming attention and specialised care in the glasshouse, practically all growers can raise a small number of cacti from seed in this manner. The only sure way to succeed is to experiment and to gain practical skills from handling the minute seedlings, and from learning about the conditions required for different cacti.

A little luck, some skill, and plenty of patience will be required and, although such a knack cannot easily be described, a few suggestions may assist those who lack practical experience in this field:

● Use small containers, made of plastic or other non-porous material, which are shallow and wide, and which can be covered by glass.

● To get the best results and strike rate, if you intend growing plants for your own seed, ensure that the seed is freshly gathered. Seeds, it is worth noting, can be stored in a cool, dry place for many months.

● Preferably construct a seed box with some bottom heat (as shown in Fig. 9); heat is an advantage at the early stages of propagation as the strike rate and growth of young seedlings is much improved. If such a structure cannot be built in time, keep the seedlings in a place which has good light and ensure that they have even heat and are not exposed to direct sunlight.

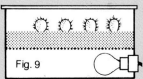

glass-top lid to maintain heat and humidity.

Grid placed some 15 cm from the top.

Fig. 9

Area below the grid heated by the bulb.

- The best time for sowing seed is in spring so as to allow for the longest possible 'growing-on' period before the onset of winter.

- If glass jars are used as containers for seedlings, they should be deep enough to allow for a base layer of fine gravel or sand (5-7cm), to allow for improved drainage from the soil above. Fill the jars with 'fine mix' soil (see Chapter 2), or crushed brick dust, to within 5cm from the top and compress lightly to provide a level surface for sowing. The soil mix should be sterilised and this can be done by partly submerging the filled glass jar in boiling water for 50-60 minutes.

- If plastic containers (ice-cream cartons, etc) are used, make pin holes through the bottoms of the containers to allow for watering and drainage. Prior to use they should be first cleansed by rinsing in hot water and then, when cool, filled with a sterilised soil mix.

- When the containers are ready for sowing, remove seeds from packet and mix with a small amount of fine sand — this will assist in more even sowing. Spread the seed/sand mixture evenly on the levelled soil and cover with a small amount of additional soil, applied through a fine sieve. Do not bury the seed too deeply. Place the containers in a shallow tray of water and allow them to soak until moisture appears on the surface. Drain away the excess water and place, if available, in a 'hot box' structure (Fig. 9) and cover with glass. (In the absence of a hot box, place in a warm location).

- Moisten the soil regularly, never allowing it to dry out completely. A gentle misting of the surface is permissable, but bottom soaking is preferable. Make sure to label each container with the relevant name of the parent plant, or from the seed packet. Note the date of sowing and, if applicable, the supplier of the seed.

A hot box can be constructed from wood with a glass top and a grid of metal or wooden laths to hold seed containers. The area below the grid should have an opening to allow for the positioning of an electric light bulb. The size of the box should be related to the bulb size and following proportions are suitable:

$\frac{1}{3}$ m³ (1 foot³) — 15 watt bulb
$\frac{1}{2}$ m³ (2 feet³) — 25 watt bulb
1 m³ (3 feet³) — 40 watt bulb.

If these proportions are adhered to the temperature within the seedlings box will remain constant at 22-25°C (70-80°F).

Watering, by bottom-soaking the seedling containers, is done outside an electrically heated box so as to avoid any danger of water coming into contact with the bulb socket or exposed flex. The temperature inside the box should be regularly checked — a thermometer should be placed inside the box for this purpose — to avoid any damage to seeds from overheating. The required amount of heat can be regulated by ventilation or, during hot periods, by switching off the power.

Depending on conditions and the type of cacti, seeds should germinate over a 3-10 week period. Not all the seeds will germinate at once, so do not be overly concerned at the initially small numbers of plants during the early post-sowing period.

Ten to 13 weeks after sowing, increase the ventilation for young seedlings by slightly raising the glass cover and allowing them to be 'aired' for 2-3 hours a day. After 18 weeks, to assist air circulation around the young plants, the glass cover can remain partially open for much of the warm part of the day. Watering, as required, can be correspondingly increased. Maintain a regular pattern of misting and bottom soaking to ensure adequate soil moisture.

Young cacti seedlings can be grafted or transplanted at an early age, usually as soon as the first spines have developed. This stage generally occurs towards the end of summer when growers with heated glasshouses transfer their seedlings into open trays.

Unless serious over-crowding occurs, I prefer to keep seedlings in their original containers over winter. In this way the transplanting and grafting can be done in early spring, and a higher survival ratio results. However, when transplanting must be done prior to winter it should be completed well before the cold weather period to allow the seedlings to get established in their new positions.

The procedures for wintering young seedlings will, in some degree, be similar to those listed for older plants. Special considerations include:

- Increased ventilation for the hardening-off period at the end of summer and a reduction of watering. However, it should be remembered that small seedlings have minimal energy reserves and too harsh conditions of wintering may result in plant loss.

- Transferring seedling containers indoors, to give them a position of good light and even temperature, is sometimes advisable. Winter temperatures should never be allowed to drop below 10°C and the soil must be kept slightly moist at all times.

- Larger, incubator-type boxes, heated by an electric bulb or some similar energy source, can also be used.

- The misting of young seedlings during fine periods is recommended.

- Limited winter growth of young plants is possible in large nurseries which have heated glasshouses. Ample light with regulated, even heating and a controlled amount of watering will be required.

Transplanting cacti seedlings into open trays involves lifting the minute plants gently from the seedling container and transferring them into prepared trays with a minimum of disturbance to the roots. A special tool can be simply fashioned from a pencil-thick piece of wooden stick, split at one end like a fork, to facilitate, without direct handling, the lifting of seedlings.

Fig. 10

Trays for the young plants are usually of a wooden or plastic type, filled with a 'fine soil' mix enriched with a small amount of inorganic fertiliser. A layer of gravel at the base (3 cm) will assist in draining any excess water.

Individual plants, or clumps of plants, are placed in rows some 2-3 cm apart and are grown-on until they reach the required potting or grafting size.

Young plants, to prevent damage from sunburn, should be shaded and kept away from direct sunlight during the hottest part of the day. At a later stage, having benefited from hardening induced by increased ventilation and exposure to light, they can be placed in positions similar to those occupied by older plants.

The watering of trays by bottom soaking is preferable to direct watering from a tap. Care should be taken not to wet the body of the plant on cold days, or just prior to nightfall. As mentioned before, misting during hot periods will be benefical as it prevents plant shrivelling and excessive drying of the soil. Adding 'Chinosol'- or a similar fungicide — to the water used for misting will assist in the prevention of mould infection in young plants and seedlings. Alkaline, tap water should never be used for watering or misting.

The wintering of one- to two-year-old cacti will prove easier for the second time around. Only limited misting during fine days will be required to avoid plant shrivelling.

Some of the more sensitive, soft-body cacti will require the more 'even' temperature of an indoor environment, or may require a limited amount of heating in a glasshouse. The more hardy types, reaching 1-2cm in diameter or more, will not have to be watered at all until the following spring .

The potting of young cacti will follow a similar pattern to the repotting of older plants. Soil should be of a 'medium coarse' type and watering is started as soon as visible growth begins. It is important not to use excessively large containers for small plants. The repotting of rapidly growing young cacti, up to twice a year, is preferable to the use of large pots.

Grafting Cacti

'To graft or not to graft' is often a hotly disputed subject among many growers. In some cases, grafting is necessary to preserve a rare or old plant which, otherwise, would not survive. The new chlorophyll-free plants from Japan — 'Yellow peanut cactus' or 'red ball' *Gymnocalycium* and similar mutants — must be grafted in order to grow at all.

Grafting is also considered essential to maintain and develop the appeal of 'cristata' or 'crest' forms of all cacti which grow in a deformed, 'comb-like' fashion. The grafting of mother plants on strongly growing rootstock also allows for more rapid propagation and the growth of many rare and difficult-to-grow genera of cacti — also old plants which have lost roots, new finds from South America, or some soft-bodied cacti like *Mammillaria, Rebutia* and others.

The slower growing cacti, or even seedlings, are grafted to speed up their development and bring them sooner to maturity and flowering stage. Some 'epiphytic' tree-growing cacti are also grafted to produce the popular 'standards' — *Zygocactus*, *Schlumbergera* and similar 'orchid' cacti.

The opponents of widespread grafting, especially on very tall stocks, argue against the rather unnatural appearance of grafted cacti — their blown-up growth pattern, which distorts their true shape and flowering. They also claim that some nurseries use stocks which enhance early growth without regard to the longer-term suitability of the match between the stock and the scion.

Much work however remains to be done in the area of the selection and breeding of suitable rootstocks which will be compatible with most cacti types. The ideal stock will resemble the scion's growth pattern, will produce a limited number of offshoots from its base and, most of all, will not 'lignify' or harden excessively with age.

The development of dwarfing stocks of lesser vigour will also benefit the growers of smaller, globular cacti by ensuring that the shape of the plants do not become distorted by excess stock vigour. Some 'cristata' forms of soft-bodied cacti — *Echinocereus* — can also suffer from over-vigorous rootstock and subsequent splitting often occurs.

The matching of a plant's vigour with its dormancy requirements and flowering period, and similar aspects, should always be considered prior to selecting a rootstock:

● The smaller, globular cacti should preferably be low grafted to maintain their natural appearance.

● The less vigorous rootstock of the *Trichocereus* type (*spachianus*), which is easy to handle, is suitable for young cacti, though the related *T.pachanoi*, as it does not harden (lignify) excessively below older plants, is often preferred as the more permanent stock.

● *Trichocereus schickendantsii* is often suitable for the regrafting or the rejuvenation of older plants, its more succulant growth increases the likelihood of successful grafting.

● Both *Cereus* and *Echinopsis* have been used in the past for rootstocks, though the vigour and hardening of the former, and the formation of numerous offshoots on the latter, can cause problems.

● *Peireskiopsis* is the most preferred rootstock for minute seedlings, its great affinity to most genera of cacti — and the rapid growth and size increase of seedlings — are reasons for its popularity. It is easy to handle and to propagate, and most of the professional nurseries use it to bring forward plant maturity. Fully grown plants are then regrafted or rooted into pots for resale.

● Species of *Selenicereus* and *Harrisia* (*grandiflorus* and *martinii* respectively), are used for the grafting of epiphytic cacti like *Schlumbergera* to form standards.

● *Opuntia* and similar segmented stocks have also been used with some success for this purpose.

● Excellent reports of seedlings grafting on *Hylocereus guatemalensis* are also known (Gardeners Chronicle, F.Hirata, 1966), and these are recommended.

In summary, it seems clear that successful

grafting will be achieved by growers who select their stock to suit both scion requirements and cultivation conditions. The rootstocks used should be in active growth — as should the scion — during the grafting period of early spring or summer. Techniques of grafting should be practised and all growers — especially the larger nurseries — should carry adequate stocks of grafting material to ensure a steady supply of rootstock at the right time.

Grafting will obviously remain an important technique for the preservation of rare species; for the growing of 'cristata' forms and for the chlorophyll-free cactus mutations. It is likely that grafting will also remain useful as an adjunct to the raising of seedlings.

It is to be hoped that widespread grafting will not be carried out as a general practice with dissimilar genera, as it is desirable that the natural appearance, growth and flowering patterns of these magnificent plants should be able to be observed in future collections.

Finally, despite the complicated appearance of the operation, cacti can be simply and successfully grafted provided that some basic rules are observed:

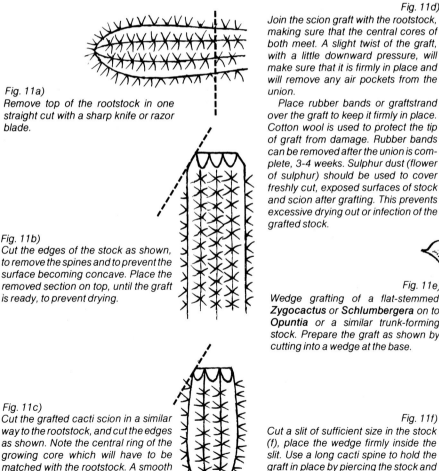

Fig. 11a)
Remove top of the rootstock in one straight cut with a sharp knife or razor blade.

Fig. 11b)
Cut the edges of the stock as shown, to remove the spines and to prevent the surface becoming concave. Place the removed section on top, until the graft is ready, to prevent drying.

Fig. 11c)
Cut the grafted cacti scion in a similar way to the rootstock, and cut the edges as shown. Note the central ring of the growing core which will have to be matched with the rootstock. A smooth surface of the cut is important to success.

Fig. 11d)
Join the scion graft with the rootstock, making sure that the central cores of both meet. A slight twist of the graft, with a little downward pressure, will make sure that it is firmly in place and will remove any air pockets from the union.

Place rubber bands or graftstrand over the graft to keep it firmly in place. Cotton wool is used to protect the tip of graft from damage. Rubber bands can be removed after the union is complete, 3-4 weeks. Sulphur dust (flower of sulphur) should be used to cover freshly cut, exposed surfaces of stock and scion after grafting. This prevents excessive drying out or infection of the grafted stock.

Fig. 11e)
Wedge grafting of a flat-stemmed Zygocactus or Schlumbergera on to Opuntia or a similar trunk-forming stock. Prepare the graft as shown by cutting into a wedge at the base.

Fig. 11f)
Cut a slit of sufficient size in the stock (f), place the wedge firmly inside the slit. Use a long cacti spine to hold the graft in place by piercing the stock and the graft it contains. The spine can be removed after union is complete.

Grafting seedlings on to stock with a large diameter.

Fig. 12a)

Prepare the stock in the same way as for grafting, with the same diameter scion, as shown in the preceding diagram. Make sure that the stock does not dry out by placing the removed section on top until the graft is ready. The stock should be growing actively during the grafting season.

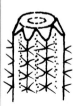

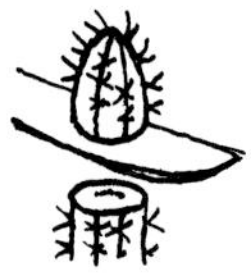

Fig. 12b)

Remove the upper two-thirds of the seedling with a sharp razor blade. Make sure that the cut is level and smooth. Do not cut the edges.

Fig. 12c)

Place the fresh scion section on to the rootstock in such a way that both central core rings meet. This is achieved by placing the scion directly across the central core-line of the stock. To prevent damage, handle the scion with maximum care.

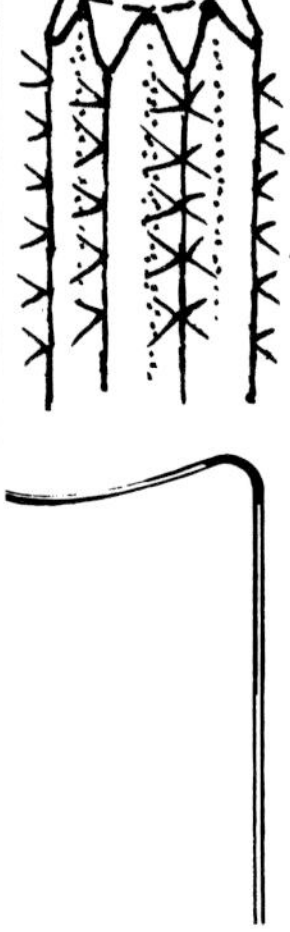

Fig. 12d)

Place the grafting spring, or a device made from a narow strip of plastic or non-corrosive metal, over the graft as shown. An anchoring stick is placed in the soil beside the plant. A small pebble can be used to hold the scion firmly in place, although it is advisable to make sure the weight is not too excessive as this could crush the soft tissues of the seedling being grafted (in many instances the weight of the strip will be sufficient). Avoid disturbing the scion for some two to three weeks until the union is complete. Allow for growth of the seedling by removing the strip after this period. Dusting with sulphur, as already suggested, is recommended.

Prevention of Damage to Cacti from Splitting and other Growth Deformations.

Aside from poor cultivation practices, discussed first, there are few, if any, serious problems which should confront less experienced growers:

● The splitting of cacti after excessive or irregular watering can be avoided by frequent, but not overly generous, watering in spring and summer. Similarly, the unhealthy and deforming winter growth of plants can be prevented by good exposure to light, cool temperatures, and by reduced watering during the rest period.

● The excessive drying out of plants is prevented by misting during fine days.

● Fertilisers, especially those that are nitrogen-rich, should always be used with caution. Splitting and anomalous growth will result from excessive nitrogen.

● Minor nutrient deficiencies (Boron etc) can occur in the well-drained, coarse soils used for cacti. Frequent repotting at yearly intervals, or the addition of a balanced nutrient mix with spring watering, usually avoids these problems.

● Older plants, large-sized, or those that are sensitive to repotting (*Melocactus* and others), should be top dressed with a well composted leaf mulch to prevent any nutrient deficiency from occuring.

Brown Scarring

This is usually caused by exposing plants to excessive heat or strong sunlight. Damage can be avoided by ventilation and by the correct placing of young and more sensitive plants in shaded positions. Brown scarring — 'mottling' — can also be caused by 'red spider' mites (described later).

Ringed Growth Deformations

These are caused by erratic watering which usually results in a stop-and-start growth pattern. The effects are mostly seen on cereoid or columnar cacti; such damage is prevented by regular watering during the growth period. Damaged plants can be restored by separating the more uniform, younger section near the top and by repotting this top portion and using the base of the cacti as a 'mother plant' for new offshoots.

Rotting and Collapse of Older Plants

When cacti lose roots, or are watered before their active and visible growth begins, the rotting of soft tissues within the plant causes a collapse and an eventual loss of the complete plant.

Keeping the soil around the roots and base of the plants wet during cold periods also results in such rotting.

Rotting can be stopped at an early stage by removing all the infected part of the roots — or the plant body — with a sharp knife, and by regrafting or rerooting the healthy section.

The yellow or reddish-brown coloured tissue is affected first by the rot at the plant centre or core — through which the main feeding veins extend. The discoloured section should be excised down to a colourless or whitish tissue.

Excessive watering of plants in winter, or splashing them with water in summer, should be avoided.

Common Insect Pests

'Red Spider' mite (*Tetranychus urticea*)
A yellow- brown mottling of cactus tissue — especially near the growing tip — often indicates damage caused by this sucking insect, a member of the mite family. On closer inspection the mites can be seen by the naked eye to be swarming in profusion — hundreds at a time — all over the plant.

Despite the common name, 'red spider' mite, much of the population observed will be of a yellow-green colour. Their red colouring becomes apparent when, as a result of excessive numbers and lack of food, the mature mites are faced with starvation. However, by then it is usually too late to prevent scarring and damage to plants.

Under conditions less favourable to the mites, their natural predators — other mites and ladybirds — control the population growth without any necessary assistance from the grower.

The hot and dry conditions which are found in many poorly-ventilated glasshouses, or along window-sills, favour a rapid multiplication of mites, and as many as ten generations of adult mites will mature in a single summer.

The regular misting of plants during hot weather, combined with ventilation and the use of insecticides, will prevent mites from damaging cacti in collections housed in glasshouses and other enclosed situations. The use of organo-phosphate based insecticides (Malathion, Maldison, Dicofol), controls mites satisfactorily, but these insecticides also eliminate the population of predator-mites so that spraying must be repeated at regular intervals.

Spraying is best done during the cooler part of the day, at two-week intervals, or as suggested by the manufacturer. As many of these systemic insecticides are poisonous to humans as well, all sprays must be kept in a safe place. Spraying outdoors should be done in calm conditions with little or no wind; the sprayer, if possible, staying up-wind of the spray. If spraying is to be carried out indoors it must be kept well away from food. All the safety precautions indicated on the label should be strictly adhered to.

The female of the red spider mite over-winter in any suitable and convenient section of the plant — the container or the glasshouse — and it is advisable to fumigate or spray all enclosed growing areas at least once in the spring, or at any time when a serious infestation occurs.

Insecticides for controlling sucking insects like mites are also available in powdered form and these may be safer to use in some situations, also it may be easier to dust the plants than to spray. Dusting should be carried out shortly after misting, as the dust will settle more satisfactorily and result in a better coating of the plants. Cacti grown outdoors are less prone to suffer from mites, although a regular inspection of young growth, and of the inaccessible sides of plants, may reveal the need for occasional spraying.

Mealy Bug (*Pseudococcus maritimus* and *P.citri*).
Another sucking insect which can cause serious damage is the mealy bug. Mealy bug infestation is easily recognised by whitish spots and a wax-like coating of wool under which the female of the species secretes herself to lay eggs. The sticky substance often hides many colonies of this insect. Dry, sheltered sides of the plant, generally between the ribs, are the most susceptible areas for initial infestation.

A number of generations of mealy bug can mature during a single season; a six to seven-week period produces a mature, female population — larger, pinkish-red, and wingless — capable of laying eggs which, once hatched, permit young insects to spread over the other parts of the plant to form new colonies.

Systemic insecticides (Malathion, Dimethoate etc) are used with success to control the mealy bug.

A minor infestation can be simply destroyed by wiping the affected areas of the plant with cotton wool dipped in methylated spirits. It is important to treat all new additions to a collection — especially older plants — against mealy bugs to prevent new infestations.

The 'root' mealy bug (*Rhizoecus falcifer*), which lives off cacti roots deep in the soil, can be more difficult to detect. By the time the grower discovers the infestation it may be too late, and a large part of the roots — or the whole plant — can be lost. Regular, yearly repotting assists in an early detection of root mealy bug and identifies plants that are in danger. Flooding the soil with systemic insecticides — and the addition of paradichlorobenzene crystals in the potting mix — are an essential part of preventive action against this parasite. As a precaution, all plants and their root systems should be inspected if they show, without an obvious reason, signs of poor growth or appear to suffer from loss of roots.

Excellent remedies are available to combat white flies and aphids which can also cause damage and regular spraying with systemic insecticides is recommended.

See Figures 13a, b, c and d for identification.

Fig. 13a)
Adult red spider mite — under 1mm in size — straw coloured and turning red when faced with starvation.

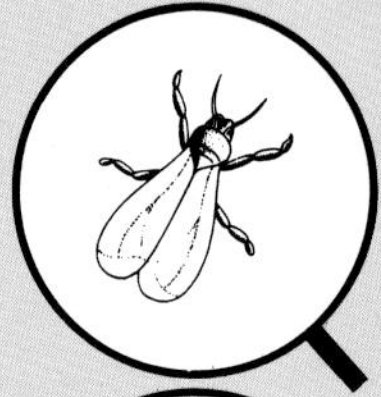

Fig. 13b)
Adult white fly — reaches 3mm in size. Damage to plants results from its oval-shaped larvae.

Fig. 13c)
Adult aphid — approximately 3mm in size. Damages plants by puncturing flower buds and young tissues near the growing tips with its pointed 'beak'.

Fig. 13d)
Adult, female mealy bug — approximately 1mm in size — without the antennae and wings of the male. Colonies of these insects protect themselves with a cotton wool-like coverage which is excreted by the female.

Mould Infections

The 'damping off' or collapse of young seedlings can be caused by a rapid growth of mould. Much seedling loss in the past can be attributed to rapid increases in alkalinity (high pH value) in seedling boxes. By bottom soaking, the salinity of the upper soil layer increases to a level where most seedlings loose their roots and become infected by mould. The use of a low-pH value 'peat' mix (see fine soil mixes, Chapter 2) or crushed brick (finely sieved) prevents much of this problem. The use of fungicide (Benlate, Chinosol, Captan etc) in watering will prevent the growth of mould.

Mould infections of freshly cut or damaged tissue, which may occur in repotting or with offset separations, can be prevented by adequate, wound healing ('callusing'). Callusing can be achieved by the exposure of cut surfaces (eg. stem or roots) to warm and dry air for a period of 7-10 days. The use of sulphur dust to prevent mould infection is recommended.

Rapid root system development can be achieved by placing the healed (callused) portion of the plant base near a water surface (see Fig. 14). This technique may be vital for the preservation of old or imported plants that have lost their roots in transit and appear to have a well lignified (hardened) base.

Any planting of insufficiently healed plants, or root, will result in infection and in subsequent plant rot. To combat mould it is important, as already recommended, to use sulphur dust to prevent infection.

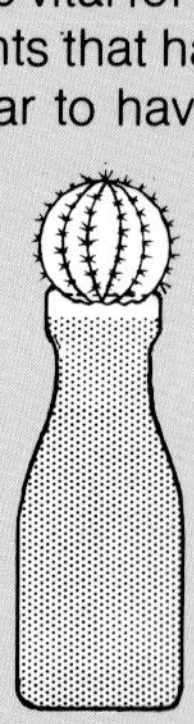

Fig. 14

Jar partly filled with water and containing a globular cacti held some 5cm above the liquid.

Terminology

The types of cacti selected for this chapter do not include all the genera and species found in nature. The plants selected, however, will give the reader an undestanding of the major groups which combine to form the family of *Cactaceae*. The list of genera included here contains those that are relatively easy to obtain and those whose body form, spines and colourful flowers, have an attractive appearance. Rare, or difficult to maintain species have been purposely excluded.

As will be seen from the descriptions that follow, a certain amount of specialised, botanical terminology has had to be included, however, the use of highly specialised terms or Latin names has been kept to a minimum.

Many growers in the course of assembling a cacti collection experience difficulties with the multitudinous attempts which have been made by various collectors and botanists to classify and re-classify these plants. New finds and new names abound and the opposing views of collectors (Britton and Rose, Rausch, Ritter and Backeberg, to mention but a few), often lead to confusion. Rather than adding to this already complex problem — which is beyond the scope of this book — nomenclature has been restricted to names in common usage and those which are generally accepted by growers and nurserymen.

Where significant differences of opinion exist, these will be referred to in the text to provide the reader with an overall appreciation of the various schools of thought, rather than as a guide to individual names. The text follows, in principle, the Curt Backeberg classification, one which is based on both plant morphology and geographical distribution. (See *The Cactus Lexicon*, Curt Backeberg, 1966 & 1976).

Names of Cacti

Both the generic name and the specific name, in that order, are included. In listing the various species of genera, the names of authors have been excluded for the sake of brevity. The collector's name and the field number should be included on the labels of all imported plants and

seed to make individual plant identification easier. This can be of assistance to all growers and collectors, as plants can be readily identified despite different classifications which may, currently, be in use.

The following genera, in alphabetical order with page numbers, are later described in detail:

Acanthocalycium *(Backeberg)*

Habitat
Small- to medium-sized, globular cacti from northern Argentina.

These are hardy plants with a preference for sunny positions, coarse soil mixes and winter rest. They can be grown well on their own roots, or may be grafted.

Body
Small to medium in size, spherical, but become slightly elongated with age. Clearly defined ribs, green to blue-grey in colour.

Spines
Usually thin and bristly, can also be short and thick. Centrals are scarcely distinguishable, and are sometimes darker tipped. The colour of spines varies from straw-yellow to dark brown.

Flowers
Blooms from mid to late summer; the flowers are large, attractive and funnelform in shape. Colours can be white, pale green-yellow, rich yellow or delicate shades of mauve and red.

A noticeable ring of wool at the base of the flower tube and the spiny scales of the flower buds are typical. Flowers rise from the crown or upper part of the body.

Propagation
Most species do not offset freely unless they are grafted. Many growers propagate from seeds with little difficulty.

Species
From the dozen or so species of *Acantho-calycium* which have been classified, the following are those seen most often in cultivation:
A.aurantiacum, A.glaucum, A.griseum, A.klimpelianum, A.peitscherianum, A.spiniflorum and *A.violaceum.*

A.klimpelianum

A.spiniflorum

A.peitscherianum

A.violaceum

A.glaucum

Astrophytum *(Lemaire)*

Habitat

One of the best known of all the cacti genera which originate from Texas and the eastern parts of Mexico.

The familiar 'Bishop's Cap Cactus' (*A.myriostigma*) is completely spineless; other species have long, flexible or rigid spines. Minute, white flakes cover the bodies of some *Astrophytum* plants, in others this is not so obvious.

All *Astrophytum* species prefer a well-drained, coarse soil mix and a dry, winter rest. A sunny position induces plentiful flowering with large and attractive blooms. All species grow well on their own roots, although grafting will increase the speed of growth in younger plants and seedlings. They prefer neutral to slightly alkaline soils and soil adjustment is achieved by the adding of small amounts of gypsum. If required, pH levels can be checked by using the litmus paper method already described in Chapter 2.

Body

Young plants are spherical to slightly elongated and of moderate size. Older plants become elongated with age and one species (*A.ornatum*) can reach one metre in height.

The body colour is green with varying amounts of white flakes, which gives some species a characteristic, greyish appearance. The few acute angles in the shape of 'Bishop's Cap Cactus' become clearly defined, other species have narrow ribs.

Flowers

Blooms are produced in mid to late summer from the woolly buds on the crown. The large flowers are in various shades of yellow, sometimes with a red centre. The plants must attain a sufficient age and size before flowering — usually after 3 to 5 years — although grafted plants will flower sooner.

Propagation

Unless grafted, offshoots are rarely seen and most growers propagate *Astrophytum* from their large seeds.

Species

From the handful classified, the following species are the best known:

A.asterias, A.capricorne, A.myriostigma, A.ornatum and *A.senile.*

A.ornatum

A.senile

A.myriostigma

A.myriostigma v.nudum

Aylostera *(Spegazzini)*

Habitat
A popular, freely offsetting and flowering genus from southern Bolivia and northern Argentina.

In more recent times this genus has been included with the closely related *Rebutia* (Ritter, Buining and others). However, Backeberg's original classification (*Kakteenlexikon* 1966), separated *Aylostera* from *Rebutia* because of differences in flower structure.

In *Aylostera*, the flower tube is always united with the *style* giving the slender tube a stem-like appearance. *Aylostera* are easy-to-grow plants with strikingly beautiful flowers. The plants prefer a coarse soil mix, full sun and a dry, winter rest. They can either be grown on their own roots or grafted.

Body
Small, spherical and soft bodied; if offsetting is allowed the heads will gradually form cushions. The ribs are formed from rows of more-or-less distinct tubercles which give these plants their characteristic appearance of perfect symmetry. The body is pale to dark green in colour.

Spines
Thin, bristly and short; straight or slightly curving. Their colour varies from silvery-white to pale or reddish-brown.

Flowers
Blooms can be expected from early to mid summer, the slender flower tube rises from the base of the plant. The flower tube tends to be hairy and bristly.

All species have brightly coloured flowers, mostly flame or carmine red and even young, two-year-old plants will flower well if cultivated under the right conditions.

Propagation
As this genus produces offsets freely, new plants can be formed readily and simply by breaking up the cushions of individual heads.

In large nurseries, seedlings are grown with little difficulty. Grafting the 'mother plants' considerably speeds up the formation and growth of offsets. *Peireskiopsis* rootstock has been used with success when making grafts.

Species
Some twenty types are listed by Backeberg; many of these, however, have been classified as *Rebutia* or *Chileorebutia* by Ritter and others. From the species which have been grown in collections the following have shown special merit: *A.albiflora, A.albipilosa, A.deminuta, A.fibrigii, A.fulviseta, A.kupperiana, A.muscula, A.maxima, A.pseudodeminuta, A.pseudominiscula* and *A.spinossima.*

A.kupperiana

A.muscula

A.fulviseta

A.pseudodeminuta

A.albipilosa

A.maxima

33

Cereus *(Millar)*

Habitat
The natural distribution of *Cereus* extends from some isolated populations in the West Indies, through the northern parts of South America, to as far as eastern Argentina and Brazil.

One of the earliest known and most widespread members of the cactus family belongs to the large genus called *Cereus*. These tall, columnar cacti grow to tree-size and have stout trunks and a crown of branches with large ribs (1). Some species of *Cereus* appear as smaller shrubs, low growing and less upright (2), but most will reach several metres in height. Because of their hardy nature and striking appearance *Cereus* cacti are well suited to outdoor culture or to large glasshouses.

In regions with severe winters, the younger plants will require protection from frosts, however, in most gardens healthy specimens can be cultivated in well-drained soils with a sunny and sheltered position near a wall, or some similar shelter from the wind.

Except for the well-known *monstrose* form of *C.peruvianus*, the plant is usually grown on its own roots.

Body
Fresh green to bluish-green in colour, usually stout and branching well above ground. The ribs are large and set well apart in exact fashion, giving *Cereus* plants their symmetrical appearance. Lower growing, bushy species also exist.

Spines
Thick and long, the central spines are often much longer and darker in colour. Usually light to dark brown — almost black — and often darker tipped.

Flowers
Flowering often occurs only after mature height has been reached. The nocturnal flowers are 20-30cm in length, many are scented and vary in colour from pure white to pink and deep red. The flower tube is glabrous, the fruit is yellowy-green or red in colour.

Propagation
Offsets from older plants and individual branches can be used. Removing the growing tip will increase the number of offsets formed, and this so-called 'mother plant' method of propagation is popular. Seeds are used by large nurseries to raise the fast-growing *Cereus* plants to saleable size in a single season.

Species
From the numberous species found in nature, the following are often seen in collections:
C.aethiops (2), *C.argentinensis* (1), *C.azureus* (1), *C.glaucus* (1), *C.hexagonus* (1), *C.peruvianus* (2) and its *monstrose* form, *C.validus* (2), *C.milesimus* (2) and *C.tacuaralensis* (1).

Pilosocereus sp. flower detail

Cereus peruvianus v.monstrosus

Cephalocereus senilis

Cleistocactus (Lemaire)

Habitat

The plants are found in central Peru, eastern Bolivia, northern Argentina, in Paraguay and in parts of Uruguay.

A large group of low-to-medium height, 'cereoid' cacti which form colonies of slender, branched shrubs. Growth is mainly upright, with many species reaching 50-150cm in height. A few *Cleistocactus* species grow taller, *C.morawetzianus* reaching several metres in height.

These are attractive plants and are admired for their fine spination of dense, bristly spines and for their flame-coloured flowers which rise in rows from the sides of each mature branch.

Cleistocacti are hardy plants and for that reason easy to grow. A well-drained, coarse soil mix, winter rest without watering, and a sunny position will suit these cacti well.

Cleistocacti are grown on their own roots.

Body

Slender, 2-5cm in diameter, with sometimes more robust stems which range from 50-150cm in height and which branch from the base to form shrubs. The shallow ribs are numerous, well defined, light to dark green in colour and are sometimes transversely furrowed.

Spines

Fine, mostly short and bristly, sometimes interspersed with longer and thicker central spines. Colouring varies from pure white, through yellow-cream to brown, centrals are often darker tipped.

Flowers

A wide range of colours from white and yellow to flame red. The flowers have a slender cylindrical tube with a narrow opening. Many species are *cleistogamic* — producing seed from unopened flowers. The base of the flower tube is always hairy.

A degree of plant maturity has to be reached — which will depend on cultivation conditions, and may take a few years — before flowering takes place.

Propagation

At home, by separating branches from the base, or by using the 'mother plant' technique and repotting the separated top. In nurseries, by seed.

Species

Including some of the more recently named finds by Ritter, the following are recommended for cultivation:

C.angosturensis, C.ayopayanus, C.baumannii, C.chacoanus, C.clavicaulis, C.crassicaulis, C.flavispinus, C.hildewinterae, C.hyalacanthus, C.morawetzianus, C.parviflorus, C.strausii, C.tarijensis, C.vallegrandensis and *C.viridiflorus.*

C.hyalacanthus

C.strausii

Coryphantha (Engelmann) Lemaire

Habitat
Their natural environment stretches from southern Canada, throughout the USA to as far south as Mexico and Baja, southern California.

Widespread in their natural habitat, the species within the *Coryphantha* genus are smallish in size, spherical to slightly elongated in shape, and are both solitary or branching in habit.

Rarely exceeding 25cm in height, these attractive plants deserve attention as they are easy to grow, flower freely and often have brightly coloured spines.

Typical of this genus are the large flowers which rise from the crown, furrowed tubercles and green, glabrous fruits. Attempts to combine *Coryphantha* with *Mammillaria* have resulted in a confusion of names and the species listed below are sometimes to be found in the *Mammillaria* section of a number of nurseries.

Coryphantha cacti can successfully be grown on their own roots, they will tolerate average conditions with well-drained, coarse soils. However, they prefer full sun and dry wintering.

Body
Small in size, often 20-25cm in height, generally spherical to slightly elongated in shape and soft-bodied with noticeably furrowed tubercles. Green to greyish-green in colour; their pattern of growth is solitary or branching from the base.

Spines
Radiating spines are usually short, interlacing and often brittle. The central spines are longer, thicker and often brightly coloured. Spines can be white, light reddish-brown or dark brown, with central spines sometimes bent at the tip.

Flowers
Blooms rise centrally from a crown which is covered with tufts of wool; the flowers are large and glossy, white, golden-yellow or red in colour, sometimes with a darker centre.

Flowering occurs from mid to late summer, with many species having to reach maturity before flowering can take place.

Propagation
Seeds are used except for those species which produce basal offsets.

Species
Although numerous species have been classified in their natural habitats, some may be listed as *Mammillarias*:
C.albicolumnaris, C.andreae, C.asterias, C.chlorantha, C.clava, C.clavata, C.cornifera, C.cornuta, C.densispina, C.difficilis, C.echinus, C.longicornis, C.minima, C.michoacanensis, C.octacantha, C.pectinata, C.radians, C.recurvata, C.speciosa, C.vaupeliana and *C.vivipara.*

C.longicornis

C.michoacanensis

C.vivipara v.neo-mexicana

C.cornifera

Copiapoa *(Britton and Rose)*

Habitat

All *Copiapoa* plants, so far named, originate from a rather limited geographical area in Chile, and many intermediate forms between the species are known.

A genus of spherical cacti which have two principal forms of growth. The first group comprises small cacti, spherical in shape and which, by offsetting, form low cushions of plants (1). The second group contains larger plants which do not offset easily and become elongated with age (2).

Natural hybridisations among a limited number of ancestral types have possibly resulted in the variations that have been observed in a number of recent finds, and it could be argued, and sometimes is, that many new names are simply forms or variants of previously known species that originated from the northern and central parts of Chile.

Copiapoas are hardy cacti, often slow-growing, however the smaller types flower freely at an early age. The taller, columnar species must often reach maturity before flowering occurs. All species are attractive, having a wide variation of colourful spines, body form and colouring.

A well-drained, coarse soil mix with a sunny position and limited watering during winter produce good growing conditions. The plants can be grafted, to speed up the growth when young, or they can be safely grown on their own roots.

Copiapoas were fashionable some twenty years ago, however they have been less comonly seen in recent times.

Body

Shapes fall into two distinct groups: small, spherical bodies forming cushions, or taller and elongated bodies which usually have a solitary form.

Body colours vary from grey to pale or dark green with shades of brown. A thick tap root is common to many species, ribs are clearly defined whether shallow or deep.

Spines

Mostly thin, long and brittle; however, thick, shorter spines — which are coloured and darker tipped — are also found on some species.

Flowers

Large in size, rising centrally from tufts of wool on the crown. The flowers have a short tube; they open wide and the petals are shades of yellow. Many species have perfumed flowers. Flowering can be expected from mid to late summer.

Propagation

Some species can be propagated by offsets. Most plants are grown from seed.

Species

The large number of species which were found and named by Ritter have recently been catalogued — thus adding considerably to the types that are available. The principal species found in collections include:
C.applanata (1), *C.bridgesii* (2), *C.calderana* (2), *C.cinerea columna-alba* (2),
C.coquimbana (1), *C.echinoides* (1),
C.haseltoniana (2), *C.humilis* (1),
C.marginata (2),
C.rubriflora (2), *C.totoralensis* (1) and
C.tenuissima (1).

C.coquimbana v.wagenknechtii

C.bridgesii

C.humilis

C.cinerea v.columna-alba

Echinocereus *(Engelmann)*

Habitat
A large group of short 'cereoid' cacti found in parts of the USA and Mexico.

Extensive variation exists between the many species of *Echinocereus*, as well as between the intermediate types that have been identified. All species are short and cylindrical in shape, they form low groups, have offsets and flower profusely.

These attractive plants, with large colourful flowers, are highly recommended and must rate as one of the most popular cacti with collectors. They are easy to propagate, relatively simple to cultivate and this, together with strikingly beautiful flowers and colourful spines, provides a combination not often seen in the family of *Cactaceae*. Dry winter rest and a medium coarse soil mix are recommended. Plants can be grown on their own roots or grafted to increase growth and flowering.

Body
Short, cylindrical soft bodies which are greyish-green in colour. They usually form colonies by offsetting at the base, however, offsets are also formed higher up the body. They customarily reach 20cm in height.

Spines
Short and soft, often 'pectinate' (comb-like), with a great variety of colours. In some species the longer centrals are darker tipped.

Flowers
Very large and attractively coloured. They flower profusely from the sides of the body and near the crown. The flower is large and funnelform with a characteristic spination and tufts of wool on the buds and base of the flower tubes.

Colours include mauve and red, often with a darker centre. Flowering can be expected from an early age and continues throughout summer.

Propagation
By offsets, which are easily detached from the mother plant, or from seed.

Species
A large number have been identified and named; a selection of the better known are given:
E.adustus, E.albatus, E.baileyi, E.blanckii, E.brandegeei, E.conglomeratus, E.delaetii, E.dubius, E.kunzei, E.melanocentrus, E.octacanthus, E.palmeri, E.pectinatus, E.pentalophus, E.procumbens, E.roetteri, E.salmianus, E.scheeri, E.tayopensis, E.triglochidiatus and *E.viridiflorus.*

E.delaetii

E. tayopensis

E.procumbens

E.tayopensis

E.palmeri

43

Habitat

A very attractive and homogeneous group of plants from northern and central Mexico.

These cacti are easily recognisable and are smallish in size. They are spherical and have many ribs — sometimes up to one hundred on a single plant. The flattened spines are typical of many species.

Given a coarse soil mix, dry winter rest and full exposure to the sun during the growing season, they can be most rewarding to grow. Attractively coloured spines and a perfect symmetry of body-form are readily apparent, even in young plants. They do not tolerate excessively dry conditions during their growing period, and misting during hot days is recommended. They can be grown on their own roots or can be grafted.

E.albatus

Body

Greyish-green in colour, with numerous ribs, often thin and wavy in appearance. The plants are relatively small in size and solitary in habit. Only a few species freely produce offsets.

Spines

Thin and long with interlacing radial spines; the centrals are often thick, coloured and flattened — even blade-like. The colour varies from cream-white to brown.

Flowers

Small or medium sized flowers rise from the crown early in spring. The flower tube is glabrous, white to violet in colour, and often displays a darker stripe. Many species flower at an early age.

Propagation

As a number of the species do not readily form offsets, plants are often propagated from seed.

Species

The more attractive species include:
E.albatus, E.arrigens, E.confusus, E.hastatus, E.lloydii, E.multicostatus, E.ochoterenaus, E.tetraxiphus, E.vaupelianus, E.violaciflorus and *E.zacatecasensis.*

E.ochoterenaus

E.tetraxiphus

E.zacatecasensis

Echinopsis *(Zuccarini)*

Habitat
The natural distribution of *Echinopsis* extends from northern Boliva, Argentina, Uruguay and Paraguay to southern Brazil.

One of the earliest of all the cacti genera to be described was the *Echinopsis*. Initially (1837) classified as a combination of several genera *Echinopsis*, *Trichocereus*, *Lobivia* and *Pseudolobivia*, it has now been accepted that these widely differing groups should be separated and classified under their own generic names. This separation was held to be valid as a result of a number of physiological as well as geographical reasons, notwithstanding the fact that it is clearly obvious from an examination of these plants that a common ancestral type exists for all of them, and for all the imtermediate types that are known to exist.

The plants classified as *Echinopsis* are generally spherical at first; with age they become elongated, at which stage they attain a short 'cereoid' shape. The differences between the shape of the flowers are seen from the description of *Echinopsis* given here, and from the similar genera which are discussed under their individual names.

The *Echinopsis* is a hardy plant, and well suited to outdoor culture. A sunny position, dry, winter rest and a fertile coarse soil mix will promote good growth and encourage more prolific flowering. The plant grows successfully on its own roots.

Body
Spherical at first, the bodies later become elongated, attaining a columnar shape and reaching up to one metre in height. Colours vary from green to greyish-green: offsets are a typical occurrence in many species.

Spines
Thick, usually short, of light colour with centrals longer and often dark tipped.

Flowers
Longer and broader than in related genera. The *Echinopsis* flower is generally funnelform and opens during the day or, sometimes, at night only.

Colours are attractive and range from white to shades of red; the flowers have a strong scent.

Some species flower at an early age, others after reaching maturity. Removing the offsets improves flowering. More prolific flowering is associated with *Echinopsis* hybrids (*Echinopsis* x *Trichocereus* and similar crosses).

Propagation
Separated offsets form roots easily. Large-scale propagation is from seed.

Species
After separating the *Trichocereus*, *Lobivia* and *Pseudolobivia* genera from *Echinopsis*, some two dozen named *Echinopsis* species remain, they include the generally more popular:
E.baldiana, E.brasiliensis, E.calochlora, E.chacoana, E.eyriesii, E.grandiflora. E.hanku-jo, E.leucantha, E.mamillosa, E.multiplex, E.rhodotricha, E.schaferi, E.silverstrii, E.turbinata and *E.werdermanii*.

One of the better known **Echinopsis** *cultivars 'Red Pygmy'.*

Detail of **Echinopsis** *sp. flower.*

Echinopsis *s.p. in outside gardens.*

Espostoa / Pseudoespostoa

Habitat

Two closely related genera of tall, columnar cacti from Peru and southern Ecuador. The natural distribution of both the plants is restricted to the higher altitudes of the Andes (some 1000-2,400m above sea level).

The separation of these two genera is not recognised by all collectors, though some significant differences in seeds, growth patterns and, most importantly, the formation of the flowering zone — the *cephalium* — can be observed.

The taller growing *Espostoa* forms a shrub by branching from the sides well above ground level. *Espostoa* seeds are without lustre and the *cephalium* is formed in a deep groove in the plant's apex. The woolly, hair-like growth which covers the plants is less dense than that of *Pseudoespostoa* and is somewhat coarse.

The *Pseudoespostoa* genus includes plants that branch haphazardly from the base, have shiny seeds and a finer, cotton-wool-like apical hair that is more dense than that of *Espostoa*. The *cephalium* of *Pseudoespostoas* does not rise from a deep groove, but resembles the 'artificial' *cephalium* of the *Cephalocereus*.

The tall and majestic *Espostoa* plants are often the crowning glory of a garden or glasshouse, their white, hair-covered columns can develop to a full height of several metres.

These are slow-growing plants, and grafting can be used to speed up the growth of young seedlings. They prefer a deep, coarse soil mix, a sheltered position, and if grown outside they may require protection from frosts.

Body

Tall, columnar plants, branching either from the base or sides (see above). The body is divided into numerous ribs, it is slow-growing and covered with a more or less dense wool growth which resembles long, white hair. The density of hair cover increases near the apex.

Spines

The radiating spines are fairly short and yellow-white in colour. The centrals are often longer, projecting through the wool and are bone coloured or browny-red. In some species the central spines are very thick and long.

Flowers

Espostoa plants have a deep groove or cleft near the apex which is clearly obvious. The *cephalium*, itself, consists of a longer, bristly growth that is considerably more dense than the surrounding wool.

Pseudoespostoa plants have a flower zone which is formed by a shallow 'artificial' *cephalium*. The flowers vary in length and are nocturnal, that is they open at night. The flower tube is hairy, white to yellow in colour, and the fruits of the *Espostoa*, when ripe, are red; whilst those of the *Pseudoespostoa* are white. Flower-bearing *cephaliums* develop on mature plants.

Propagation

This genus can be propagated from offsets, the 'mother plant' system, or from seed.

Species

Espostoa:
E.huanucensis, E.lanata, E.mirabilis, E.mocupensis, E.procera and *E.ritteri*.

Pseudoespostoa:
P.melanostele and *P.nana*.

E.ritteri f. cristata

E.lanata

E.mocupensis

E.huanucensis

Gymnocalycium (Pfeiffer)

Habitat
Gymnocalycium is a large and extensively culti-vated genus of cacti from Bolivia, Paraguay, Uruguay, southern Brazil and Argentina.

It was first mentioned as a separate genus in 1845 and since then it has become one of the most popular cacti with growers in all countries.

These are hardy plants of small to medium size and spherical in shape. The tuberculate ribs, glabrous flowers, and fruits with their distinctive scales are typical of all *Gymnocalycium* species.

Usually they do not demand special attention or a particular soil type, though winter rest and a semi-shaded position on the cooler side of a glasshouse — as well as plentiful watering during the growing season — are recommended. They can be grafted, although they grow well on their own roots.

Body
A very small to medium-sized body, always spherical and becoming slightly elongated with age. The body is formed by rows of tuberculate ribs that are more, or less defined, depending on the species. The body colours range from greyish-green to variegated shades of green and reddish-brown.

Natural mutation under cultivation in Japan has, in recent times, produced plants that lack chlorophyll — the so-called 'red ball cactus' or the *G.mihanovichii* mutant — which has to be grafted in order to survive. Some species offset freely, others do not.

Spines
Variation in both colour and size is great. Spines can be curved close to the body, often interlac-ing and projecting to form a dense cover. Some varieties have short and straight spines, others have longer centrals which are attractively coloured: yellow, brown, or shades of red.

Flowers
Most species flower freely from early to late summer — even at an early age. Flowers rise from top of the tubercles, near the areol, and have scales on the flower tube and buds. In size the flowers vary from very large to small; they have slender tubes, are funnelform in shape and have many attractive shades of colour, ranging from white and yellow to pink and red. Glabrous fruits are typical.

Propagation
More usually from seed but can be raised from offsets where small numbers of plants are re-quired.

Species
From the great number of attractive species the following are most often found in collections:
G.andreae, G. anisitsii, G.asterium, G.baldianum, G.bicolor, G.bodenbenderianum, G.bruchii, G.cardenasianum, G.damsii, G.denudatum, G.gibbosum, G.griseo-pallidum, G.hamatum, G.horridispinum, G.hossei, G.hybopleurum, G.kozelskyanum, G.leeanum, G.mihanovichii, G.multiflorum, G.mostii, G.ochoterenai, G.quehlianum, G.saglione, G.spegazzinii, G.stuckertii, G.vatteri and *G.zegarrae.*

G.baldianum

G.leeanum

G.quehlianum v. zantnerianum

G.mihanovichii v. friedrichii

G.horridispinum

G.multiflorum

Hamatocactus *(Britton and Rose)*

Habitat
A genus of small, spherical cacti from Texas and northern Mexico.

All species have narrow ribs slightly swollen around the areols and large, glossy yellow flowers.

The plants are easy to grow and prefer a coarse soil mix, full sun and winter rest without watering. They can be grown on their own roots and flowering can be expected with young plants.

Body
Small, spherical, becomes slightly elongated with age and green to greyish-green in colour. Clearly defined, narrow ribs. The plants rarely offset, except when the growing tip becomes damaged.

Spines
Thin and bristly, the central spines are longer, lighter tipped and off-white in colour. Some centrals are always hooked and are slightly reddish, radial spines are straight.

Flowers
Large and in attractive shades of golden yellow with a sheen. Some flowers have a red centre. Buds are green in colour, scaly, and rise from the top of areols near the crown.

Flowering occurs with quite young plants in mid summer. Flowers are 5-7cm long and open fully to over 6cm in diameter.

Propagation
By seed as, unless grafted or damaged, offsets rarely form.

Species
From the handful of *Hamatocactus* which have been classified the following are the best known: *H.hamatacanthus, H.setispinus* and *H.sinuatus*.

H.setispinus

Helianthocereus (Backeburg)

Habitat
A genus, closely related to *Trichocereus*, containing two distinct groups of cacti from northern Argentina and Bolivia.

The first group comprises tall, columnar plants which are found at higher altitudes in the Argentine Andes. These plants branch from the base, have thick stems and are several metres in height. The flowers appear near the tip of mature shoots (1).

In the second group the plants are considerably smaller, low-growing and form bushes with branches which do not reach more than a metre in height. The second group of *Helianthocereus*, the group described here, are of more interest to growers who are limited in space to a verandah or glasshouse (2).

Flowers of the low-growing *Helianthocereus* appear from the sides of the stems, are large and attractively coloured. The plants are hardy and can be grown outdoors: they prefer a position of full sun. Winter rest, without watering, and a cool winter climate induce better flowering characteristics. They can be grown on their own roots.

Body
Low-growing shrubs of slender stems, clearly ribbed. The colour varies from shades of green to grey. The stems reach up to one metre in height and branching occurs from the base.

Spines
Fairly thick with centrals often longer and dark tipped. The colour varies from yellow to light brown.

Flowers
Large, funnelform with a distinctively hairy tube. The flowers are attractively coloured and glossy, in shades of yellow or flame red, they stay open for a few days, closing at night.

Sizes range from 10-12cm in length and 6-7cm in diameter. The buds are hairy, brown in colour, and appear laterally, often low on the stems.

Propagation
Usually by offsets or from seeds.

Species (2)
A number of attractive species have been classified and the following are of interest:
H.crassicaulis, H.grandiflorus, H.huascha, H.hayalacanthus, H.pecheretianus and *H.pseudocandicans.*

H.huascha

Lobivia *(Britton and Rose).*

Habitat
A very large and outstanding group of cacti from Bolivia, central Peru and Argentina.

Possibly the most admired, the most intensively studied and the most widely collected of all cacti. The *Lobivias* were superbly described by Walter Rausch in his book, *Lobivia: the day flowering Echinopsidinae*, published by R.Herzig in Vienna.

Lobivias are relatively small plants: some are solitary and become elongated with age, but most are offsetting and form cushions of 'barrel-shaped', or spherical heads.

The flowers are uniformly funnelform, large but with a short tube (see *Echinopsis*), and open during the day. *Lobivia* flowers achieve an astonishingly great range of colours — every shade of cream and yellow to brillant red, with all shades in between.

All *Lobivias* grow well on their own roots, although grafting is often used to speed up growth and to increase flowering. This is possibly the most highly recommended type of cacti for those who wish to start a collection.

All species are hardy and with protection from an excess of rain they can be grown outside. They prefer a medium coarse soil mix with full sun and plentiful watering during the growing season. Plants require a dry rest in winter.

Body
Mostly small and spherical, some solitary and elongated with age. They form cushions of numerous offsets, all are clearly ribbed and green to greyish-green in colour.

Spines
Vary from very short and pectinate (comb-like), to thick and elongated, often attractively coloured. The spines can be yellow, brown or red and centrals are often longer and dark tipped.

Flowers
Plentiful, large and attractively coloured. Funnelform in shape, some up to 10cm long and 6-7cm wide. Buds and flower tubes are hairy, with flowers rising from the lower mid-section of the body.

Flower colours range from white and yellow to all shades of red, often with darker centres.

Flowers can be expected from young plants.

Propagation
Usually from offsets which can be separated from older plants during the repotting stage. Seed propagation is used by larger growers and nurseries.

Species
A great number of species have been classified, those listed are among the finest to be found in collections:

L.akersii, L.aurantiaca, L.backebergii, L.boliviensis, L.cardenasiana, L.culpinensis, L.famatimensis, L.fricii, L.hastifera, L.hystrix, L.jajoiana, L.multicostata, L.neocinnabarina, L.planiceps, L.shaferi, L.simplex, L.tiegeliana, L.vanurkiana, L.vatteri, L.wagneriana and *L.winteriana.*

L.famatimensis v. leucomalla f.rubrispina

L.famatimensis v. densispina s.v. blossfeldii

L.shaferi

L.backebergii

L.planiceps

L.silvestrii (s.g. Chamaocereus)

Lobivia / Chamaocereus

Chamocereus silvestrii is a well-known and freely flowering species of the *Lobivia* genus from the mountainous regions of northern Argentina which was previously classified as *Cereus*, later as *Chamaocereus*, and finally as *Lobivia* in 1967.

W. Rausch, an Austrian cacti collector and authority on *Lobivia* supported this final classification and showed the close relationship of *Lobivia silvestrii* to the other species within the *Lobivia* group, specifically the similar *Lobivia saltensis*.

The popular *Lobivia silvestrii* is a rapidly growing, short 'cereoid' plant which under conditions of cultivation tends to offset freely and to form clumps of short stems which, in their turn, bear numerous flowers.

New crosses with other *Lobivias*, sometimes known as *Chamaelobivia*, have thicker stems and therefore tend to break up less easily.

55

Mammillaria *(Haworth)*

Habitat

The natural distribution of *Mammillaria* extends from the southern states of the USA, through Mexico to Guatemala, Honduras, Venezuela, the West Indies, northern Colombia and Curacao.

With some 350 species already named, *Mammillarias* comprise the largest genus in the *Cactaceae* family and there seems little doubt that collectors will discover new species in the years to come.

The name *Mammillaria* is derived from the Latin diminutive of *mamma* — *'mamilla'* (a nipple-shaped organ), thus giving the more correct name of *'Mamillaria'* which is common to some countries (Backeberg, Salm-Dyck and Schumann support this nomenclature).

The uniform characteristic of all *Mammillarias* are tubercles arranged in intersecting spirals which replace the ribs which are found in many other types of cacti.

A similar arrangement can also be seen in the sub-genera of *Dolicothele* and *Krainzia* — a situation which has resulted in attempts by some collectors to combine these genera under one name.

The *Mammillaria* flowers are small, rising in ring formation from the 'axils' (depressions between the tubercles), and are often accompanied by a ring of wool. The plants are usually small to medium size, spherical or elongated and cylindrical, with or without milky sap. The thick or bristly spination is often short and colourful. The smaller species have central spines which are generally hooked, and they also have larger flowers.

A great majority of the species are easy to grow, and comprise hardy plants that prefer full sun, a medium to coarse soil mix and a dry, winter rest. They often grow well on their own roots; however, some of the smaller, soft-bodied species are grafted as they can easily lose their roots.

Body

Small or elongated with a spherical to cylindrical shape, habits are both solitary and offsetting. Colours vary from fresh green, through grey to red. Typical of this genus are spirals of intersecting tubercles (*mamilla*), and a woolly growth in the ring-shaped flowering zone.

Spines

Short, bristle-like and colourful in many species; projecting rigid spines, with longer centrals — which can be hooked — are also seen in the smaller varieties.

In a few species the spination is reduced to a soft, feather-like growth of hair (*M.plumosa*), giving the plants a delicate, thistledown appearance. The colour of the radial spines varies from a whitish-yellow to reddish-brown, the centrals are often darker tipped.

Flowers

Rising from the axils, in rings around the upper part of the body and crown, small to large, bell-shaped with a short tube. A woolly growth in the flowering zone is a typical characteristic of this type of cactus.

Colours range from white, cream, yellow and pink to dark red and mauve, often with a darker stripe. The plants with large flowers (*M.boolii* and others) can be more difficult to maintain but are well worth cultivating because of the bloom size and colour. Flowering can be expected with young plants.

Propagation

On small scale by offsets or, if being raised in quantity, from seed.

Species

The more attractive species generally seen in collections include:
M.albicoma, M.albilanata, M.blossfeldiana, M.bocasana, M.bombycina, M.boolii, M.camptotricha, M.calacantha, M.celsiana, M.centricirrha, M.collinsii, M.compressa, M.confusa, M.dealbata, M.diacentra, M.discolor, M.dixanthocentron, M.elegans, M.elongata, M.fuscata, M.guelzowiana, M.geminispina, M.glassii, M.hahniana, M.hertrichiana, M.ingens, M.kraehenbuehlii, M.lanata, M.louisae, M.magnifica, M.mainae, M.meissneri, M.microhelia, M.mollendorffiana, M.nana, M.nejapensis, M.perbella, M.plumosa, M.pringlei, M.rhodantha, M.ruestii, M.saint-pieana, M.schiedeana, M.spinossima, M.supertexta and *M.wilcoxii.*

M.(s.g. Krainzia) guelzowiana

M.boolii — front M.nana — back

M.rhodantha

M.celsiana

M.dealbata

Mediolobivia *(Backeberg)*

Habitat
The natural environment stretches from Bolivia to northern Argentina.

One of the most floriferous groups of cacti which, because they are small and easy to maintain, have become popular with growers all over the world.

Mediolobivias range from spherical to short-cylindrical plants, they offset to form cushions of individual heads. Spination is colourful and the flowers have brillant colours and, like *Rebutia* and *Aylostera*, rise from the base of the plant.

Some collectors group these three genera under one name; however, clearly defined differences in the structure of the flowers exist, thus supporting the contention that the three genera should be separated (see Backeberg 1976).

The ribs of *Mediolobivias* are formed by thin and slender rows of tubercules, and the flowers have a distinctive ring of wool at their base. All species are easy to grow and require a medium coarse soil mix, dry winter rest and plentiful watering during the growth period.

Grafting can rapidly increase the size of the seedlings, but the plants will grow and flower well on their own roots.

Body
Small, spherical to short and cylindrical in shape, greyish-green to bronze coloured and often forming cushions from offsets. The slender ribs are clearly divided to form the tubercles.

Spines
Bristly, thin and long, usually straight, or interlacing and dense at the base of the plant. The colour of the spines varies from light brown to darker reddish-brown.

Flowers
Plentiful, even with young plants; the flowers rise from hairy buds which sometimes carry bristly spines. The buds form in a ring shape around the base of each head.

The splendid *Mediolobivia* flowers are funnel-form, large and brightly coloured. They range from yellow and white to golden-orange and flame red. Flowering can be expected from early to mid summer.

M.schmiedcheniana v. einsteinii

Propagation
By individual offsets or by seed.

Species
Some of the following may be found under *Aylostera* or *Rebutia* names in literature (Rausch and Ritter):
M.albopectinata, M.aureiflora, M.brachyantha, M.brunescens, M.elegans, M.eos, M.FR1118, M.ithyacantha, M.pectinata, M.pygmaea, M.ritteri and *M.schmiedcheniana.*

M.FR 1118

M.brachyantha

M.aureiflora v. rubelliflora

M.ithyacantha

Melocactus *(Tourneff)* Link and Otto

Habitat
One of the earliest cacti to be imported into Europe was the so-called 'melon-thistle' or 'melanodistel', a species of **Melocactus** from Mexico. It is also found in the West Indies, Honduras, Guatemala, central Peru and northern Brazil.

The *cephalium* bearing **Melocactus** are not easy to grow or maintain and, with older plants which bear the 'bristly' *Cephalium* crown, special care must be taken to avoid root loss.

Grafted seedlings grow well in warm glasshouses with higher than usual levels of humidity. Similar growth conditions can be created in an old-fashioned 'glass garden' made from an upside-down, large jar or an inverted glass fishtank.

Maintaining summer warmth (above 20°C) and high humidity (above 75%) is important. The soil mix should be medium coarse with an increased humus content and should not be allowed to dry out completely, even in winter.

Because of their sensitive root systems, *Melocactus* plants should either be grafted or cultivated with a minimum of repotting.

Older plants bearing the *cephalium*, instead of being repotted, should be placed in a sufficiently large pot and top dressed with a leaf mulch and nutrients. It is important that plants grown on a glasshouse bench should receive regular misting.

Body
Spherical at first, but becomes elongated with age; some species do form offsets. All species form a bristly, *cephalium* crown from which the flowers rise. The body is formed from a few large ribs which can be greyish-green or bluish-green in colour.

The root system is sensitive to repotting and care must be taken, especially with older plants, not to disturb the ball of roots.

Spines
Thick radial spines with longer centrals which protrude and are slightly bent at the tip. Colours range from tan and yellow to brown or red.

Flowers
Small and bell-shaped with a short tube. They rise in a ring formation from the woolly *cephalium* on the crown.

Although small, the flowers are attractively coloured often in shades of orange and flame red. Plants must reach a mature size before the *cephalium* is formed, this is usually some 5 to 7 years from the seedling stage.

Propagation
Offsets are not formed readily and plants are raised from seed. It is recommended that young plants should be grafted.

Species
The following more attractive species are commonly seen in larger collections:
M.albicephalus, M.amoenus, M.amstutziae, M.azureus, M.bahiensis, M.communis, M.ernestii, M.macrodiscus, M.matanzanus, M.melactoides, M.peruvianus, M.rubrispinus, M.ruestii and *M.violaceus.*

M.rubrispinus

M.bahiensis

M.ernestii

M.amstutziae

Neochilenia (Backeberg)

Habitat

A large genus of Chilean cacti, classified separately by Backeberg from *Neoporteria* and *Horridocactus* (two similar genera) because of its broadly funnelform flower which always shows recognisable hair growth on the flower tube.

The distinction between *Neochilenia* and *Horridocactus* also appears justified on geographical grounds as the ancient barrier of the Andes comes between the two genera.

Some authors, notably Ritter, argue against the separation and some of the species named here may, in other places, be listed as *Chileorebutia*, *Neoporteria* and *Horridocactus*.

Full sun, a coarse soil mix and dry winter rest are important for all *Neochilenia*. They are hardy plants, usually small and sometimes even dwarf in size, although a few will reach a greater size and become elongated with age.

They can be grafted to speed up growth, however they will all grow well on their own roots. Typical growth in the smaller species includes tuberculate ribs and hairy flowers and fruits. All the species have woolly areols and open funnelform flowers.

Body

Usually small, spherical and greyish-green to dark brown in colour. The ribs are formed by rows of tubercles. The elongated, larger plants have longer, straight ribs.

Spines

Mostly straight, short and thin, with longer centrals which are bent up or down. The colours vary from grey to near black.

Flowers

Appear from woolly buds on the crown. Flowers are funnelform; they open fully and their short tubes are always hairy.

Colours range from white and yellow to red. The flowers are medium sized and attractively set among the longer spines.

Propagation

Mostly from seed as, without grafting, the formation of offsets is not commonly seen.

Species

Numerous species have been classified as members of the *Neochilenia* genus by Backeberg. Some of those listed here have been named *Neoporteria* and *Horridocactus* by Ritter and other collectors:

N.atra, N.calderana, N.chilensis, N.dimorpha, N.floccosa, N.glaucescens, N.gracilis, N.mitis, N.napina, N.nigriscoparia, N.paucicostata, N.pygmaea, N.reichei, N.scoparia, N.taltalensis and *N.wagenknechtii*.

N.paucicostata

N.pygmaea

N.atra

N.napina

Neoporteria *(Britton and Rose)* Backeberg

Habitat
A very uniform group of cacti originating from central to northern Chile; the spherical to slightly elongated (cylindrical) plants bear a chacteristic flower with up-turned curving, inner petals.

This unvarying and unique flower characteristic separates *Neoporteria* from the similar but geographically distant genera of *Neochilenia* and *Horridocactus*.

Some authors unite all three under the one name, *Neoporteria*, and species listed elsewhere (see *Neochilenia*) may be listed as *Neoporteria*. (Ritter, Britton and Rose and Hutchinson).

Neoporterias are attractive plants, with fierce spination and distinctive flowers. A coarse soil mix, dry winter rest and full sun make for successful growing and will ensure that the plants are bought to their best flowering condition.

Well suited to outdoor culture, *Neoporterias* are hardy and very popular with growers — especially the lower-growing, spherical types which tend to flower more freely. The grafting of seedlings is widely used to bring the young plants sooner to a mature, flowering size. Older plants grow well on their own roots.

Body
Either small and spherical, or short cylindrical and elongated with age. The clearly defined ribs are swollen near the areols to form 'chin-like' tubercles.

The body colours range from greyish-green to dark green, and most plants are solitary in habit and do not form offsets.

Spines
Fierce, and often thick with noticeably longer centrals which are darker in colour and up- or down-turned.

In a few species (*N.gerocephala*), the spines are reduced to thin and dense bristles which cover the whole body. The colour of the spines varies from tan to brown and near black.

Flowers
These are uniform for all species and retain their unique shape. The inner petals are up-turned and curving.

The flowers are wax-like and glossy, ranging from delicate pink to flame red in colour. Flowering occurs with young plants, especially if they have been grafted. the flower buds are pointed, slender and rise from areols near the crown.

Propagation
From offsets formed on grafted plants or, more usually, from seed.

Species
N.castanea, N.clavata, N.gerocephala, N.litoralis, N.microsperma, N.nidus, N.nigrihorrida, N.planiceps, N.robusta, N.sociabilis, N.subgibbosa, N.villosa and *N.wagenknechtii.*

N.microsperma

N.nidus

N.nigrihorrida v.coquimbana — left
N.gerocephala — right

N.villosa

65

Notocactus *(K. Schumann)* Berg

Habitat

Notocactus are found in Argentina, throughout Uruguay and in southern Brazil.

An attractive and easy to grow genus which is to be seen in most nurseries and collections. They can be successfully grown under most conditions, and flowering is easily achieved, even with young plants. The plants are spherical to oval in shape with distinctive spination and attractive, large, glossy, yellow flowers.

Optimum growing conditions include a medium coarse soil mix, sunny position and plentiful watering during summer. The young plants flower even when small; some *Notocactus* species will considerably increase their size and become oval with age, others which are slow-growing, will remain relatively small. Plants are usually grown on their own roots.

Some of the species may be found under the related, sub-generic names of *Malocarpus*, *Eriocactus* or *Brasilicactus*.

Body

Small, spherical to oval in shape, the numerous ribs are clearly defined. The body colour varies from fresh green to bluish-green and reddish-brown.

Most species have a chin-like swelling around the areols, from which the spines rise.

Spines

Can be thick at the base and long, with distinctive centrals, or bristly-thin with bright colours. Pale yellow and reddish-brown spines are a typical feature of the *Notocactus*.

Flowers

Large, funnelform flowers rising from the crown. The buds and flower tubes are covered with wool, the flower petals are glossy and are usually yellow in colour.

A red flowering-species (*N.uebelmannianus*) is also known. Early to mid summer is the usual flowering time.

Propagation

Some species offset more readily than others, however they can all be propagated with little difficulty from seed.

N.muricatus

Species

N.apricus, N.buiningii (s.g. Malocarpus), N.floricomus, N.haselbergii (s.g. Brasilicactus), N.herteri, N.horstii, N.leninghausii (s.g. Eriocactus), N.mammulosus, N.megapotamicus, N.muricatus, N.ottonis, N.roseoluteus, N.rutilans, N.scopa, N.submammulosus, N.tabularis, N.uebelmannianus and *N.werdermannianus*.

N.uebelmannianus

N.(s.g. Brasilicactus) haselbergii

N.(s.g. Eriocactus) leninghausii f.cristata

N.horstii

N.werdermannianus — front
N.herteri — back

Opuntia *(Tourneff)* Millar

Habitat
The natural distribution of *Opuntia* extends from Canada, the West Indies and the Galapagos Islands to parts of southern Argentina.

Some species of *Opuntia* can be found in North Africa, the Mediterranean region of Europe and in Australia (modern introductions).

This is the second largest genus in the *Cactaceae* family, with species which have a great variety of forms ranging from the largest (1), tree-like plants to low, prolifically branching species (2) which can be grown in pots or in mini gardens. Regardless of their size, *Opuntias* always show an abundance of flowers and can have most attractive spines.

Hardy in nature, and often bizarre in shape, the plants are very suitable for outdoor cultivation in gardens or on a verandah.

Winter watering should be kept to a minimum. However, during summer months, all the larger species benefit from regular watering.

Some *Opuntias* (Prickly-pear), bear attractive fruits which are edible and, in their native habitat they are collected and sold in the produce markets.

It is not necessary to graft *Opuntias* as they will grow and flower equally well on their own roots.

In the past some nurserymen have grouped together a number of *Opuntia*-related genera under the same name, however in recent years only those plants with characteristically flat, circular, stem segments are included. Others, like *Cylindropuntia*, *Austrocylindropuntia*, *Nopalea* and *Tephrocactus* have been classified as distinct genera and sold under their appropriate names.

Body
Bizarre in shape and segmented into flat, circular stems. They vary in size from miniatures to bush-like cacti (2) and large trees reaching over four metres in height (1). The segments are grey to fresh green in colour and some separate easily.

Spines
White, or coloured in shades of red and brown. They can be long and thick at the base, although in most species the spines are short and detach easily. The barbed 'glochids' can be seen on young stems.

Flowers
Often an abundance of flowers which rise along the perimeter of mature segments.

The flowers vary from funnelform to cylindrical in shape and are large and glossy; colours range from yellow to red with all shades in between. Fruits are grey-green in colour and red when ripe.

Propagation
Easily propagated by planting individual segments, or by seed.

Species
From among the many *Opuntia* species found in nature the following merit space in a collection:

O.abjecta (2), *O.aciculata* (1), *O.armata* (2), *O.azurea* (2), *O.basilaris* (2), *O.compressa* (2), *O.ficus-indica* (1), *O.fragilis* (2), *O.galapageia* (1), *O.grandiflora* (1), *O.hystricina* (2), *O.longispina* (2), *O.macrocentra* (2), *O.microdasys* (2), *O.occidentalis* (1), *O.penicilligera* (1), *O.phaeacantha* (1), *O.polyacantha* (2), *O.rhodantha* (2), *O.robusta* (1), *O.stricta* (2), *O.sulphurea* (2), *O.tomentosa* (1), *O.tuna* (2), *O.vulgaris* (1), *O.vulpina* (2) and *O.wilcoxii* (1).

Opuntia sp. flower.

O.robusta

O.tuna

Oreocereus (Berg) Riccobono

Habitat

A hardy genus of strongly hairy plants from northern Argentina, Bolivia, southern Peru and Chile.

Oreocereus plants usually form low groups of slender columns with distinctive, coloured spines and long, hair-like tufts of wool. Flowering occurs only with older plants, the flowering zone, pseudo-cephalium, is sub-apical (near the crown).

The hollow fruit is yellow-green in colour, and opens at the base to expose the black seeds. This characteristic is unique amongst the Cereus genera and was the main reason for classifying Oreocereus as a separate genus. However, differences of opinion still exist about this point and some collectors include Oreocereus among other genera, e.g. Morawetzia and Borzicactus (Kimnach and others).

In its native habitat the woolly growth protects the cacti at higher altitudes from excessive amounts of radiation from the sun (as with Espostoa, Cephalocereus and other similar genera of cacti).

The length and amount of wool varies amongst the Oreocereus species, sometimes it is short and close to the areols, at other times it is long, covering most of the body.

Although slow in growth, these cacti are an attractive addition to even the smallest of collections.

A coarse soil mix, dry winter rest and a position with full sun will suit these plants well. They grow well on their own roots, however seedlings are often grafted so as to increase their size more rapidly. Their display of colourful spines and woolly growth provides a fine background to all the smaller, spherical cacti.

Body

Columnar branches form low groups (1); the taller species reach several metres in height (2), although many are considerably shorter. Ribs are clearly defined and greenish-grey. All species have tufts of wool growth in varying lengths.

Branching occurs at the base or, very rarely, above the base.

Spines

Short, radiating spines, white in colour; long thick centrals project from the wool and vary in colour from yellow to shades of orange and red.

Flowers

Flowering occurs from the sub-apical zone, just below the crown; the flower tubes are long and cylindrical with narrow openings.

The flowers are cleistogamic, i.e. self fertile, and do not open fully.

The fruits are yellowy-green; spherical in shape and open at their base. Colours range from pink to deeper shades of red. Flowering can be expected only with older plants. The flower length is close to 8cm.

Propagation

By individual branches, or by stems which can be separated from the base at the repotting stage.

In larger nurseries, Oreocereus are propagated from seed.

Species

From the handful of species of Oreocereus (remembering that some growers may have these listed as Morawetzia or under other names), the following are often seen in collections:
O.fossulatus (1), O.maximus (2),
O.neocelsianus (1), O.trollii (1) and
O.variicolor (2).

O.neocelsianus

O.trollii

O.maximus

Parodia (Spegazzini)

Habitat
A large group of globular to elongated cacti from Bolivia, northern Argentina, Paraguay and Brazil.

Most species of *Parodia* are easy to grow, they flower prolifically and present few problems to the majority of growers. They are often grafted to increase flowering, although they grow and flower well on their own roots.

Parodias are an attractive, symmetrical cacti, often with a fierce spination which is yellow or red, straight or hooked. A coarse soil mix and dry, winter rest is essential. The best spination and flowering is seen on plants grown outdoors in open-air frames.

With age many *Parodia* species become elongated and some growers prefer to maintain the plant's spherical shape by, every 7 to 10 years, cutting off the head in the spring and re-establishing it as a new plant.

Apical wool, colourful spines and free flowering are a very typical feature of this interesting genus of cacti.

Body
Fresh green to grey in colour, *Parodias* are spherical to oval in shape. With age the body becomes thicker and more elongated. Ribs are more or less defined by rows of tubercles. Unless the growing tip is damaged, most species do not offset freely. Short growths of apical wool near the areols are common.

Flowers
A short flower tube with wool; the brightly coloured flower petals varying from glossy yellow to shades of red and violet. The flowers rise from woolly buds in a ring formation near the crown.

Spines
Radiating spines are mostly short and whitish-yellow in colour. The centrals are longer and projecting, sometimes straight, more often hooked or up-turned. Radiating spination is dense and interlacing.

Propagation
By offsets from damaged 'mother plants' or from seeds.

Species
From the thirty or so named species which occur in nature, the following receive most attention by growers:

P.aureicentra, P.aureispina, P.backebergiana, P.borealis, P.camargensis, P.carminata, P.commutans, P.compressa, P.elegans, P.formosa, P.fulvispina, P.gracilis, P.jujuyana, P.maasii, P.microsperma, P.mutabilis, P.penicillata, P.rubida, P.rubriflora, P.salmonea, P.stuemeri, P.subterranea, P.superba, P.suprema and *P.yamparaezi.*

P.maasii

P.aureispina

P.yamparaezi

P.rubriflora

P.subterranea

Pseudolobivia *(Backeberg)* Backeberg amended

Habitat
The natural environment stretches from the Bolivian Highlands to northern parts of Argentina.

A group of cacti closely related to *Echinopsis* and the *Lobivia* group which was given a separate classification by Backeberg on the grounds that its flower shape was a natural, intermediate step between the short, day-flowering *Lobivias* and the relatively tall night-flowering *Echinopsis* (see Backeberg 1976).

This view is not uniformly accepted and many collectors and authors prefer not to recognise an intermediate stage and to list the *Pseudolobivia* species mentioned in this section as *Lobivia* or *Echinopsis*. Rausch, Ritter and Britton and Rose, for example, do not acknowledge the use of *Pseudolobivia* as a separate name.

In order to avoid any confusion it should be emphasised that the species listed in this section are those identified by Backeberg as belonging to a separate classification.

A confusion in nomenclature notwithstanding, plants sold as *Pseudolobivias* are well worth growing and are easy to maintain.

Spherical to slightly elongated in shape, *Pseudolobivia* plants have large (*lobivoid*), brightly coloured flowers and spines.

A coarse, fertile soil mix, dry wintering and plentiful sun and water in summer will suit these plants well. They are usually grown on their own roots and are recommended to all growers.

Body
Spherical, medium sized and fresh-green to greyish-green in colour. Some species become elongated with age (like *Echinopsis*), others remain spherical, reaching some 30cm in diameter.

Many do not offset readily unless the growing tip is damaged.

Spines
Short, straight, radiating spines; in some species the centrals are longer, thick and attractively coloured. One or two species have hooked centrals.

Flowers
Long tubes (not as long as *Echinopsis*, longer than *Lobivia*).

Brightly coloured flowers of yellow, light and deeper red with a few species having white flowers like *Echinopsis*. In most species the flowers open during the day, however night-flowering species also occur.

The buds rise from depressions on top of tuberculate ribs near the crown, or 'apically' - often with a characteristic ring of wool at the base. Flowering takes place in mid to late summer.

Propagation
As many plants do not offset easily, most growers propagate from seed.

Species
From Backeberg's classification the following *Pseudolobivias* are of interest:
P.aurea, (=Lobivia)*, P.carmineoflora (=Lobivia), P.kermesina (=Echinopsis) P.kratochviliana (=Lobivia), P.luteiflora (=Lobivia), P.orozasana (=Echinopsis) P.potosina (=Lobivia) P.rojasii (=Echinopsis) and P.wilkeae (=Lobivia).

* classification according to Rausch is shown in brackets.

P.aurea

74

P.kermesina

Rebutia *(K.Schumann)*

Habitat

A large genus of small, soft bodied cacti from northern Argentina and Bolivia.

The *Rebutias* are very popular with nurserymen and growers alike because of the ease with which they grow and can be propagated, and for their flowers.

The numerous flower buds appear during early summer in a ring formation around the plant's base and it is not uncommon to see a young *Rebutia* with twenty and more flowers at once — each flower twice the size of the whole plant!

Rows of tubercles form the more or less spiralling *Rebutia* ribs, giving the plants a very symetrical appearance.

Rebutias are easy to raise providing their soft body is protected from excessive moisture by a coarse soil mix; they require a dry winter rest and should be watered only during their active growth period. They grow well on their own roots, however they are often grafted to speed up the growth of young seedlings and to bring forward flowering.

In many ways the *Rebutia* genus is similar to the *Sulcorebutia*, *Mediolobivia* and *Aylostera* group (see each genus for descriptions), and sometimes the *Rebutias* are sold under any one of these names.

Glaborous scales on the flower tube are typical for all *Rebutias*.

Body

Small and soft bodies with symetrical rows of tubercles forming ribs. The body colour varies from fresh green to darker shades of green. Offsets are formed each year to form cushions of small heads, each bearing flowers.

Spines

Soft, bristle-like, short and straight with scarcely differentiated centrals. Sometimes interlacing and pointed upwards, dense white-grey spination round the areol is a typical characteristic.

Flowers

Attractive and plentiful — even with year-old plants. Flower buds rise in a typical ring formation from the plant's base.

Flowers are funnelform, have short tubes and are bright in colour. The flower tube has glaborous scales, sometimes very distinct, at other times less so.

The flowers are usually slender and mostly flame red or yellow in colour.

Some species are self fertile and readily form glaborous fruits which dry out to expose numerous black seeds. Flowering usually takes place from early to mid summer.

Propagation

Easily propagated by separating the cushions of offsets, or from seed.

Species

From the many species collected in their native habitats, the following have most merit:
R.calliantha, R,chrysacantha, R.glomeriseta, R.graciliflora, R.grandiflora, R.krainziana, R.marsoneri, R.minuscula, R.senilis, R.violaciflora, R.wessneriana and *R.xanthocarpa.*

R.senilis v.kesselringiana

R.senilis v.lilacino-rosea

R.glomeriseta

R.krainziana

R.grandiflora

Sulcorebutia (Backeberg)

Habitat
A genus of spherical cacti from north-eastern Bolivia closely related to *Rebutia*. In general growth and flowering they resemble *Rebutia*, however they have thicker spination, a large tap root and narrow, elongated areols on the top of tubercles that taper upwards.

The free formation of offsets, seen in *Rebutias*, is not so common — although grafted plants form offsets more readily.

Numerous species, previously listed as *Rebutia*, were re-classified as *Sulcorebutia* and these, in addition to the new species, have increased to over forty the numbers available.

Popular with growers, *Sulcorebutias* are usually slightly larger than the small *Rebutias*, they have fierce and colourful spines and, like *Rebutias*, flower freely.

A medium coarse soil mix and a position with full sun, combined with a dry, winter rest, suit *Sulcorebutias* well. They can be grown well on their own roots, although they are often grafted to speed up growth and to increase flowering.

Body
Small and spherical in various shades of green and brown. A thick tap root and up-turned tubercles are typical.

Spines
Borne on characteristically lengthy, linear areols, the *Sulcorebutia* spines are often fierce and long, the centrals are projected and are interlacing.

Some species carry spines which are short and bristly with no centrals, or only ones that are scarcely differentiated. The colour of the spines ranges from white and yellow to shades of red and brown.

Flowers
Simple, large and resembling those of a *Retubia*. Slender and funnelform in shape, the flowers often rise from the lower part of the body. Flowering takes place from early to mid summer.

Colours range from orange and flame red to yellow.

Propagation
Unless grafted, offsets are not formed readily and propagation from seed is often used.

Species
From the large number of species named to date, the following show merit in cultivation: *S.alba*, *S.breviflora* (previously as *Rebutia brachyantha*), *S.candiae*, *S.crispata*, *S.flavissima*, (previously as *Lobivia hoffmanniana*), *S.hoffmanniana*, *S.kruegeri* (previously as *Aylostera kruegeri*), *S.markusii*, *S.mentosa*, *S.muschii*, *S.polymorpha*, *S.steinbachii*, *S.tarabucensis*, *S.taratensis* (previously as *Rebutia taratensis*), *S.tiraquensis*, *S.tunariensis* (previously as *Rebutia tunariensis*), *S.vasqueziana* and *S.weingartiana*.

S.weingartiana

S.tunariensis

S.hoffmanniana

S.steinbachii

S.mentosa

Thelocactus *(K.Schumann)* Britton & Rose

Habitat
A distinctive group of spherical cacti from Texas and Mexico.

Moderate in size, **Thelocactus** plants have colourful, long spines and large, brightly coloured flowers. They are relatively easy to cultivate in most positions and a coarse soil mix, a sunny exposure and a dry, winter rest will suit them well.

The plants are usually grown on their own roots and rapidly reach maturity and flowering size. Tuberculate ribs, with elongated areols and scales on the glaborous flower tube are typical.

Body
Spherical, to slightly elongated with age, greyish-green to fresh-green in colour. The ribs are formed from rows of tubercles that are elongated near the flowering zone on the crown.

Some species offset from the base, others do not.

Spines
Radiating spines are short, straight, and often white. The centrals are longer, also straight, but often coloured brown, red or yellow.

In some species the central spines are flattened and flexible, most are rigid.

Flowers
Large, opening fully to 10cm in diameter and brightly coloured. Shades of pink, red or purplish-mauve, often with darker centres, are customary. The flower tubes and buds are glaborus, carrying scales.

Propagation
Usually from seed, however some species offset readily.

Species
From those found in their native habitat the following are popular:
T.bicolor, T.flavidispinus, T.heterochromus, T.hexaedrophorus, T.leucacanthus, T.nidulans and *T.wagnerianus.*

T.bicolor

T.nidulans

T.wagnerianus.

T.leucacanthus v. schmollii

T.heterochromus

Trichocereus *(Berg.)* Riccobono.

Habitat
A large group of columnar cacti whose natural environment stretches from Ecuador to Central Argentina and Chile.

The plants reach a height of several metres (1), or form lower colonies of slender branches (2).

Some species of *Trichocereus* resemble the taller-growing *Echinopsis* in their growth form.

The spectacularly large *Trichocereus* flowers are nocturnal and some remain open the following day as well.

Trichocereus are hardy plants, well suited to an outdoor position in a sheltered, sunny corner of a garden. If given full sun, well drained, fertile soil and protection from wind, the taller species can enhance even the smallest of gardens.

The plants are usually grown on their own roots.

Body
Generally tall, columnar branches (1), offsetting at the base. The ribs are clearly defined with a dark to fresh-green colour. Also low growing, forming colonies of slender branches (2).

Spines
Vary from short and bristly to thick, long and rigid. The centrals are often longer and darker tipped. Spine colours range from yellow and brown to dark brown.

Flowers
Large, funnelform, reaching some 15 to 25cm in length. The flowers have hairy tubes - slender or thick — opening in the evening and closing during the morning of the following day. Some species flower for longer periods, although this rarely exceeds a day or two.

The flower colours range from white and pink to deeper red; often the flowers are perfumed.

The fruits are green, or reddish in colour when ripe, and are generally spherical in shape and covered with hair.

Propagation
Can be grown from offshoots; from 'mother plants', from sections of stems or, in larger nurseries, from seed.

Many species (*T.spachianus*, *T.pachanoi*, *T.schickendantzii* etc) are useful as rootstocks for other cacti.

Species:
T.candicans (2), *T.carmarguensis* (2), *T.cephalomacrostibas* (1), *T.chilensis* (1), *T.fulvilanus* (1), *T.glaucus* (1), *T.grandiflorus* (2), *T.neolamprochlorus* (2), *T.pachanoi* (1), *T.peruvianus* (1), *T.schickendantzii* (2), *T.smrzianus* (2), *T.spachianus* (1) and *T.thelogonus* (1).

Trichocereus flower detail.

Mature specimens of Trichocereus in cultivation.

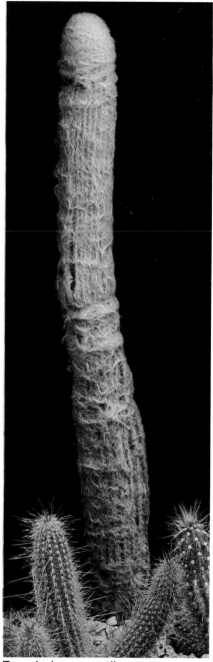

T.cephalomacrostibas

T.thelogonus

Zygocactus and other Epiphytes (K.Schumann

Habitat

From Brazil, and possibly the best known and most widely cultivated group in the *Cactaceae* family is the *Zygocactus* — usually sold as 'Christmas Cactus' or *gliederkaktus*.

Some confusion exists in reference books on cacti as to its relationship with *Epiphyllum* (an old and well-used name meaning 'leafy cactus'), *Schlumbergera, Rhipsalis* and other epiphytic cacti groups which have different segments and flower structure.

It is accepted, however, that *Zygocactus* (syn. *Epiphyllum*) has short segments, flowers with long, true-corolla tubes and lengthy, projecting anthers. The inner series of filaments are united and become a short tube at the base of the flower tube.

A typical fruit is distinguished by an extremely unusual shape which bears some resemblance to an old-fashioned spinning top and which rests on the remains of the spherical ovary (for further details on morphology see Backeberg 1976).

Schlumbergera, on the other hand, is an almost extinct genus which is found only in cultivation, not in nature. Other similar types of 'orchid' or epiphytic cacti are the *Rhipsalis* varieties — all of these require cultivation conditions which differ from those which are suitable for ground or 'terrestial' cacti. However, all the epiphytic or 'tree-growing' cacti from the warm climates of the Amazon basin share a requirement for humus-enriched soil mixes (peat and leaf mulch), combined with higher temperatures in winter and all-the-year-round moisture.

An ideal summer position would be outdoors (a shaded veranadah or under a large tree), in ground which has plenty of moisture and is phosphorus-rich with a low pH value.

Hanging baskets are often used with success for this type of cacti.

Plants are brought indoors for winter flowering, and these should be placed in a well-lit position with constant sun and a temperature of about 15-17°C.

Watering is maintained throughout the winter, or pots containing epiphytic cacti can be placed in larger containers partly filled with a mild nutrient solution and water.

Significant changes in exposure to light, ie. turning the pot, or in temperature — as in a heated room — can result in flower drop.

Plants benefit from regular misting when brought indoors.

Body

Formed by a series of small segments, which are spineless, rounded and with more or less pronounced teeth along their margins.

The plants form low shrubs with long branches of up to 30cm. The body colour ranges from fresh green to darker shades of green.

Spines

A few bristles of pale white colour.

Flowers

Rise apically from the ends of the mature segments in winter, hence the name 'Christmas Cactus'. The flowers have long, slender tubes; petals curve outwards and filaments protrude well outside the flower tube.

Colours range from pink and deeper carmine to violet-blue. In size they vary from 6 to 8cm in length and 3 to 4cm in diameter. Orange flowered hybrids with atypical flower arrangement can also be bought. There are usually *Zygocactus* x *Schlumbergera* crosses.

Propagation

From individual segments which are grown as new plants on hot-beds in a glasshouse; the temperature and humidity levels must be increased to ensure satisfactory propagation.

Species

Zygocactus species
Z.truncatus.

Schlumbergera species
S.russelliana.
A plant sold under the name *S.bridgesii* is a hybrid.

Rhipsalis species
R.aculeata, R.boliviana, R.burchellii, R.cassutha, R.cereoides, R.clavata, R.crispata, R.elliptica, R.heptagona, R.jamaicensis, R.linearis, R.madagascarensis, R.pilosa, R.roseana, R.teres and *R.wercklei.*

Rhipsalidopsis species
R.rosea.

Schlumbergera (Lemaire), Zygocactus
Rhipsalis (Gärtner), Rhipsalidopsis (Britton and Rose), Selenicereus (Berg)

Plants sold as *Rhipsalidopsis Gärtneri* are identical to *Epiphyllopsis Gärtneri*.

Selenicereus species
A group of climbing (epiphytic) cerei with large, nocturnal flowers. All species require the high temperature and humidity of a heated glasshouse. The natural distribution extends from eastern Mexico and the north coast of South America to the West Indies and Cuba.
S.brevispinus, S.coniflorus, S.grandiflorus, S.maxonii, S.pringlei, S.pteranthus, S.urbanianus, S.vaupelii and *S.wercklei*.

'Queen of the Night', the night-flowering *Selenicereus grandiflorus*.

flower detail

R.roseana

Zygocactus x Schlumbergera hybrid.

Epiphyllopsis Gärtneri

APPENDIX:
Cactus and Succulent Societies and Journals

Great Britain

National Cactus and Succulent Society
Membership Secretary: Miss W.E. Dunn, 43 Dewar Drive, Sheffield.

Journal of the Cactus and Succulent Society of Great Britain
Secretary: 67 Gloucester Court, Kew Road, Richmond, Surrey.

USA

Henry Shaw Cactus Society
Secretary: Mrs C. Maurier, 6651 Antire Road, High Ridge, M.O. 63049.

Cactus and Succulent Journal
Abbey Garden Press, 1675 Las Canoas Road, Santa Barbara, California 93105.

Further Reading

Andersohn, *Cacti and Succulents,* E. P. Publishing 1983

Backeberg, *Cactus Lexicon,* translated by L. Glass, Blandford Press 1976

Barthlott, *Cacti: Botanical Aspects, Descriptions and Cultivations,* translated by L. Glass, S. Thornes 1979

Bechtel, *Cactus Indentifier,* Blandford Press 1981

Britton and Rose, *The Cactaceae,* Dover Publications 1937

Busch, *Cactus in the Desert,* Crowell, New York 1981

Buxbaum, *Cactus Culture,* translated by V. Higgins, Blandford Press 1958

Campton, *Cactus Garden,* J. G. Miller 1967

Cook and Ivimey, *Introduction to Cacti and Succulents,* Cactus and Succulent Society 1978

Cutak, *Cactus Guide,* Van Nostrand Reinhold 1976

Ginns, *Cacti and other Succulents,* David and Charles 1975

Glass and Foster, *Cacti and Succulents for the Amateur,* Blandford Press 1977

Higgins, *Cactus Growing for Beginners,* Blandford Press 1954

Innes, *Cacti,* Royal Horticultural Society 1978

Innes, *Cacti and other Succulent Plants,* Ward Lock 1979

Innes, *Complete Handbook of Cacti and Succulents,* Ward Lock 1980

Jacobsen, *Lexicon of Succulent Plants,* Blandford Press 1977

Kramer and Worth, *Cacti and other Succulents,* Abrams 1979

Lamb, Edgar and Brian, *The Illustrated Reference on Cacti and other Succulents, Volume One,* 5th edition, Blandford Press 1975

Lamb, Edgar, *The Illustrated Reference on Cacti and other Succulents, Volume Two,* 3rd edition, Blandford Press 1973

Lamb, Edgar and Brian, *The Illustrated Reference on Cacti and other Succulents, Volume Three,* 2nd edition, Blandford Press 1963

Lamb, Edgar and Brian, *The Illustrated Reference on Cacti and other Succulents, Volume Four,* 3rd edition, Blandford Press 1975

Lamb, Edgar and Brian, *The Illustrated Reference on Cacti and other Succulents, Volume Five,* Blandford Press 1978

Lamb, Edgar and Brian, *Cacti in Colour,* Blandford Press 1969

Lamb, Edgar and Brian, *Colourful Cacti and other Succulents of the Deserts,* Blandford Press 1974

Lamb, Edgar and Brian, *Pocket Encyclopaedia of Cacti in Colour including other Succulents,* Blandford Press 1981

Martin and Chapman (eds.), *Illustrated Guide to Cacti and Succulents,* Salamander 1982

Mulligan, *Cacti and Succulents,* Frederick Muller 1979

Rausch, *Lobivia, the Day Flowering Echinopsidinae,* translated by J. Donald, Rudolf Herzig 1975

Riha and Subik, *Illustrated Encyclopaedia of Cacti and other Succulents,* Octopus 1981

Schonfelder and Fisher, *Illustrated Guide to Cacti and Indoor Plants,* translated by E. Launert, H. Starke 1972

Scott, Stanley and Henderson, *Observer's Book of Cacti and other Succulents,* Frederick Warne 1981

Shewell-Cooper and Rochford, *Cacti as House Plants, Flowers of the Desert in your Home,* Blandford Press 1973

Subik, *Concise Guide to Cacti and Succulents,* Hamlyn 1969

Taylor-Marshall and Woods, *Glossary of Succulent Plant Terms,* Abbey Garden Press 1945

Glossary

Glossary of Technical Terms

Acariasis: infection by mites.

Acicular: slender needle-like body, needle-like spines or bristles.

Acute: sharp at the end, coming to a point.

Anomalous: unconformable, deviating from the usual.

Anther: the pollen sac carried on top of each filament.

Apex: the upper side of the tubercle from which the flowers or wool arise.

Apiculate: ending in a short and sharp tip, having a minute apex.

Appressed: flattened against another part of the plant as in spine; held closely.

Areole(s): in cacti the specialised area from which the spines, wool or flowers rise, the cell nucleus of the plant.

Articulate: jointed or having a node (joint).

Ascending: curling upwards, as in spines or flower petals.

Assimilation: a process of plant metabolism by which simple sugars (assimilates) are produced in the green parts of a plant — such as the leaf or stem — which contain chlorophyll. Sunlight (energy), carbon dioxide (from the atmosphere) and moisture (supplied by the roots), are all required for this.

Assymmetrical: lacking regular shape, with parts not arranged correspondingly.

Axil: where the upper side of the leaf joins with the stem or tubercle.

Banded: marked with stripes of colour.

Bract: a flattened scale-like appendage to another organ.

Berry: a simple fruit with fleshy pericarp (seed-vessel).

Binominal nomenclature: a system of botanical nomenclature introduced by Linnaeus (1707-1778). Plant names are classified by a minimum of two words — the generic name and the names of the species.

Bristle: stiff hair or very fine, soft flexible spine.

Calcareous: chalky, rich in lime; usually a soil type with an alkaline reaction (above pH7).

Cespitose: growing in tufts or clumps.

Callus: a hardened plant tissue which forms over a wound or cut.

Calyx: the outer ring of the parts of a flower, a floral tube or cup.

Campanulate: bell-shaped flower.

Capsule: a dry, dehiscent seed vessel composed of two or more parts (carpels).

Carpel:	pistil-cell, whether pistil is one cell or several. The modified leaf in which are produced the ovules, the individual constructive, physiological unit of the plant body.
Central spine:	the spine(s) rising from the centre of the areole, usually protruding and distinct from an outer ring; they are longer or coloured in most cacti.
Cephalium:	a head of hair-like growth on the top or side of a cactus from which the flowers rise.
Chlorophyll:	the green pigment in plants. Essential for *photosynthesis*.
Cleistogamous:	pollination and fertilisation taking place in an unopened flower.
Columnarius:	of the nature or form of a column, columnar.
Compressed:	flattened shape.
Corolla:	the inner ring of the parts of a flower consisting of the petals, usually brightly coloured.
Cotyledon (di-):	a seed leaf, forming part of the embryo of a seed. The first leaf to develop when a seed germinates (dicotyledonous — possessing two cotyledons).
Cristatus (cristate):	crested, forming a fasciated condition, compressed and massed together (relates to shape).
Cruciform:	shaped like a cross.
Cutting:	a vegetative part of the plant used for propagation.
Cylindric:	cylinder-shaped.
Decumbent:	reclining towards the ground, but with an upwards pointed tip.
Dehiscence:	the opening of ripe fruits to expose seeds.
Dimorphic:	having two distinct forms.
Diurnal:	of the day; flowers opening only during the day.
Echinocarpus:	having spiny fruits.
Ellipsoid:	a compressed oval shape (a solid of which all the plane sections through one of the axes are ellipses, and all other sections ellipses or circles).
Endemic:	regular, found in a specified region.
Epidermis:	the outer cell layer of a plant.
Epiphyte:	a plant growing on (but usually not nourished by) another plant.
Family:	botanically, a group of one or more similar genera — usually ends with *aceae* (i.e. *Cactaceae*). Similar families are grouped into an order.
Fasciation:	a malformation of plant stem, resulting in a flattened, massed and enlarged crest (found in *cristata* forms of cacti).
Filament:	the stalk which supports the pollen sac (anther).
Funnelform:	a flower shape created by an upwardly widening flower tube.

Genus:	botanically, a subdivison of a family, consisting of one or more species which show similar characteristics and appear to have a common ancestry. Plural genera.
Glabrous:	smooth-skinned, without hair or spines.
Globose:	shaped like a globe; spherical, or nearly so.
Glochid:	a barbed hair or bristle (as with *Opuntia*).
Habitat:	the natural home or environment of a plant or animal.
Holotype:	the original type specimen used in defining a species.
Hybrid:	the offspring of a cross between plants of unlike genetic constitution.
Imperfect:	applied to flowers in which any normal part is wanting — a flower that lacks either stamens or pistils (male or female parts respectively).
Lacerate:	having deep and irregular cuts along the edges or point.
Lacteus:	of the nature of milk, refers to sap which resembles milk, as in *Mammillaria*.
Lanate:	having a long, soft, woolly covering, as in *Epostoa*.
Lanceolate:	like a spear-head in shape, tapering.
Lineate:	marked with stripes or lines.
Mamilla:	nipple-shaped organ or protuberance; a tubercle, for instance.
Monoecious:	having separate male and female flowers on the same plant.
Morphology:	the science of form; botanically the structure and form of plants.
Mutabilis:	not consistant, changeable.
Mutation:	a sudden variation in the hereditary material of a cell.
Mutant:	a plant which has acquired a heritable variation as a result of mutation.
Nocturnal:	flowers that open at night only.
Oblique:	having sides which are unequal or assymetrical.
Obovoid or ovate:	egg-shaped, with narrower end forming the base.
Offset:	a side shoot, or lateral branch, which has a growing tip and can produce a new plant.
Ovary:	the reproductive organ in which seeds (ovules) are formed after pollination.
Ovule:	the part of the ovary of a plant containing the egg cell which, after fertilisation, develops into a seed.
Pectinate:	to fit together in alternation like the teeth of a comb: shaped like a comb with parallel spines.
Perennial:	a plant which continues growth from year to year.

Perianth:	the outermost, non-sexual part of a flower which encloses the stamens and pistils, usually comprising the calyx and corolla.
Persistent:	remaining attached.
Petal:	modified leaf of the corolla, usually the coloured part of a flower.
Photosynthesis:	the process by which green plants synthesise carbohydrates from water and carbon dioxide, using energy from sunlight which is absorbed by *Chlorophyll* in the green tissues.
Pilose:	with a covering of slender, soft hair.
Pistil:	the female, (seed bearing) part of a flower, comprising the ovary, style and stigma.
Plant cell:	the basic structural unit of all plants.
Plumose:	feather-like, as in the spines of *M.plumosa*.
Porrect:	extended horizontally.
Prostrate:	growing along the ground.
Pruinose:	frosted, covered with wax-like bloom.
Radians:	radiating spines, extending in a circle from the areols.
Recurved:	spines bent fully backwards.
Rib:	the primary vein of a leaf, in a cactus the parallel ridges or rows of tubercles that form the body.
Rootstock:	plant material with good rooting properties onto which material with desirable vegetative features is grafted.
Rotate:	botanically, wheel-shaped, especially of a corolla which is a single petal with a short tube and spreading limb.
Scale:	a modified leaf on the ovary, flower tube or bud of a cactus. A flattened membranous, more-or-less circular plate of cellular tissue, usually a rudimentary or degenerate leaf.
Septum:	a dividing wall or partition.
Species:	a group of closely related plants, bearing similar characteristics, that intercross freely. A subdivision of a genus. The species forms the second part of the plant's botanical name.
Spine:	a pointed, rigid or bristle-like part of the cactus, a modified leaf.
Stamen:	the pollen-bearing (male) part of the flower, comprising *anther* and *filament*.
Stigma:	the portion of the pistil (female part of the flower) which receives the pollen.
Stoma:	a small breathing pore on the leaf or stem of plants. Plural stomata.
Style:	the stalk-like portion of the pistil, connecting the stigma with the ovary.
Succulent:	any plant that has water storage tissue in the leaf, root or stem.

Symmetrical:	a shape that can be divided into two identical halves.
Synonym:	a new name given to a plant incorrectly, as it has been previously named.
Systemic disease:	a disease in which a single infection results in a spread of the disease throughout the whole plant.
Systemic fungicide:	a fungicide which is absorbed by the plant and moves in the sap to all parts of the plant.
Tomentose:	Covered with down or dense, woolly hair.
Tube:	A hollow cylindrical channel, the united basal portion of the flower.
Tubercle:	A conical protuberance which carries an areole, as in *Mammillaria* or *Coryphantha*.
Truncate:	Ending abruptly as if cut off at the tip — the leaf of *Zygocactus truncatus*.
Type locality:	The place from which the type specimen was collected.
Variety:	A group of plants within a species or subspecies which share similar characteristics, but which differ in respect of those characteristics from other groups within the species. Also used to indicate an improved variant of a cultivated plant — a cultivar.
Vascular bundle:	tissue in the centre of the plant stem comprising a cluster of strands which conduct water and minerals from the roots to the plant.
Xerophyte:	Plants, such as cacti and succulents, which are adapted to survive on a limited supply of water.
Zygomorphic:	Symmetrical about a single plane, divisible into similar lateral halves in only one way, as in *Zygocactus*.

Index